I'll Fight...

Holiness at War

Phil Wall

Sovereign World

Sovereign World Ltd
PO Box 777
Tonbridge
Kent TN11 0ZS
England

ISBN: 1 85240 223 7

This Sovereign World book is distributed in North America by Renew Books, a ministry of Gospel Light, Ventura, California, USA. For a free catalog of resources from Renew Books/Gospel Light, please contact your Christian supplier or call 1-800-4-GOSPEL.

Cover: original design by Jim Moss adapted and re-drawn by Susi Dodds.
Typeset by CRB Associates, Reepham, Norfolk.
Printed in England by Clays Ltd, St Ives plc.

Dedication

Dedicated to Captains Geoff and Sandra Ryan, for holding before me a model of our founding dream.

My thanks must go to the many people who have helped with this project. To Andrew Miles and Adrian Gosling for their help with the writing and initial editing; to Gill Jordan for typing much of the manuscript; to Chris Mungeam of Sovereign World for your belief in the book; to Dave Hoyle, my first youth leader for trusting me with leadership; to John Dangerfield, my boss, who believed in me enough to take a risk (and still does). To the Mission Team and members of Raynes Park Community Church who journey in faith with me. To those who have written recommendations for the book and for your mentoring influence upon my life. To Steve Chalke for having an ever open door. To Andy Hickford for asking the awkward questions. To Steve, Diane, Jack and Jill for investing in my marriage. To General Paul Rader for writing the fore-word and for his visionary leadership. To The Salvation Army for allowing me to serve. To Ian Mayhew who has shaped my life and continues to call me on by his example. To Russell Rook my assistant and friend for his faithfulness. To my best friend and wife Wendy and children Jake and Yasmin for your love and patience. Finally to God for loving and accepting someone who finds it easier to be an ambassador than he does a child.

Contents

Contents

Definition of Terms
Theology of Fanaticism
Conclusion

Changing World
The Role
The Challenge

Preface

'And now, comrades and friends, I must say good-bye. I am going into dry-dock for repairs, but the Army will not be allowed to suffer, either financially or spiritually, or in any other way by my absence; and in the long future I think it will be seen – I shall not be here to see, but you will – that the Army will answer every doubt and banish every fear and strangle every slander, and by its marvellous success show the world that it is the work of God and that the General has been his servant ... While women weep as they do now, I'll fight; while men go to prison, in and out, as they do now, I'll fight; while there is a drunkard left, while there is a poor girl lost upon the streets, while there remains one dark soul without the light of God, I'll fight – I'll fight to the very end!'

These are the final public words spoken by William Booth, founder of The Salvation Army. He and his wife Catherine and those that rallied around them, began a spiritual revolution that has touched the lives of millions since that day. Their aggressive and passionate spirituality was stabilised and strengthened by a strong commitment to the doctrine and experience of holiness. This is one of the most distinguishing marks of salvationism. William commented that '...only this, it seems to me can justify us in having any separate existence.' The fusion of a military, fighting metaphor with a spirituality centred upon inner sanctification and transformation that manifested in public demonstration, was a glorious marriage that has spawned many spiritual children around the world. This was truly *Holiness at War*.

It is the contention of the author that in many places around The Salvation Army world, as well as within the wider church, a divorce of these two has taken place. This has left us with a military metaphor stripped of much of its meaning and devoid of its power to transform the lives of individuals and send them out to transform their world. It has also left us with a doctrine of holiness that has become for many a shallow expression of personal piety manifesting itself in a legalistic adherence to rules and regulations, an impotent religiosity shrouded in denominational allegiance. For either of these two 'estranged' partners to have any sense, meaning, or valid identity, they must be re-married at the altar of obedience with the reciting of the words 'what God has joined together, let man not separate'.

I am someone who believes that the best days of The Salvation Army are not behind us but could be ahead of us. Yet many of my peers and those of the younger generations have grown up with a hybrid form of salvationism that has struggled at times to make sense of our identity, matching the historical roots with the current day reality. This future is not guaranteed but heavily dependent upon our ability to see this 'great divorce' of metaphor and doctrine reconciled. These are not unique concerns of Salvationists, but rather issues that need to be considered by all earnest believers who want their lives to count for God. Though the consistent point of reference for these concerns is in a Salvation Army context the core challenges are much broader. The gaps between our creeds or song lyrics and the reality of our lives, are ones that need to be bridged.

One of the aims of this book is to place The Salvation Army doctrine of holiness back into its warfare context, thus enabling the founding dream of this Movement to be more fully realised.

Foreword

There is something bracing about this book. The freshness of its appeal, the passion with which it pulses, the vision it boldly casts for a stripped-down, Spirit-directed and disciplined fighting force focused on final victory. Still, the passionate rhetoric that rings from these pages will make more than a few readers edgy. Listening to prophets, especially young ones, has never been a particularly comfortable exercise – nor is it intended to be. But passionate spirituality is in short supply in our apathetic age. And prophetic integrity, the more so. We do well to pay attention – to recognise its vital importance to us in The Salvation Army and in the Church of Jesus Christ. *'Welcome with meekness the implanted word that has power to save,'* James advises, as *'doers of the word and not hearers only'* (James 1:21–22 NRSV).

What Phil Wall says so compellingly makes sense of the Army's radical rhetoric that echoes an earlier and more chauvinistic age, and yet, was never more urgently relevant, in the face of the ever-intensifying spiritual struggle of our time to resist the stranglehold of Satan on so much of our cultural experience. This is not a time for comfortable Christianity. There is too much at stake. Too much to be lost. Too much to be gained. The Church of Jesus Christ – this Army of God – is under mandate to fight, until our conquering King comes in glory to claim his Kingdom. And so, this trumpet blast!

It is time to unmask and face down the *'ruler of the power of the air, the spirit that is now at work among those who are disobedient'* (Ephesians 2:2). Evil, like a noxious gas pervades the moral ecosphere. Our greatest threat is not anthrax in the water supply, but a spiritual apathy that allows sin to pollute the vital sources of our cultural understanding. This generation is subject to a continuous media message that intends to induce a deadly drowsiness and to make mush of our moral faculties, subtly subverting our faith in the biblical values and standards by which we have assumed our lives to be guided as Christians. No wonder Scripture warns: *'Wake up! ... Be very careful how you live ... making the most of every opportunity, because the days are evil'* (Ephesians 5:14–16). Or, as *The Message* translation has it: *'These are desperate times!'* And desperate times call for desperate measures – out of a desperate devotion to Jesus Christ and the cause for which he went to the limit – death on a Cross!

Phil Wall writes out of his Salvationist heritage and appeals first to fellow Salvationists to reconnect with their Founder's call to selfless spiritual conflict. But in these pages every believer will be brought face-to-face with what it means to live out a soldier's covenant as a warrior for God in a godless world where grace and goodness, truth and justice, are inevitably conflictual.

Read with an open mind and a hearing heart. You'll not be the same, if you do.

General Paul A. Rader
London, England
1998

Introduction

The young priest bowed his head to open his weekly service. People took up the customary position recognised the world over as prayer, yet this was to be a service like no other that day. He began his opening doxology as he lifted his head and looked out over the 'worry weary' heads of his assembled congregation. This was a land where glasnost was still a distant dream and people came to church for comfort and hope in a society that lacked both.

As the priest opened the Bible, the pious silence was broken as the doors at the rear burst open and a group of menacing militia came storming into the church screaming for everyone to stay seated. Each carried a Kalashnikov rifle, and the group of eight took up position around the perimeter of the pews with one at the front and back. Children began to cry, adults looked around in fear and bewilderment and the young priest quaked as he tried to calm his assembled flock.

The attention of the men was drawn to the back as a tall man entered through the doors and strode arrogantly down the centre aisle. He sneered at the young priest and ignored his somewhat limp and pathetic enquiry as to what was happening, then turned and addressed the crowd. 'We are a Secret Police unit.' Panic began to possess the people at the sound of the feared arm of the secret police. 'You have a very simple choice this morning and that is to stay or leave . . . ' Confusion mixed with the fear as the man spoke. ' . . . very simply in five minutes time we are going to shoot any Christian left in this building.' As the chill words filled the air two of the soldiers loaded their guns and the click of the ratchets echoed around the sanctuary. The priest tried to object but drew back as the squad leader glared at him in a way that left no doubt as to the inherent threat.

Children cried, men and women screamed as bodies began to flood out of the building leaving behind bags and coats in their urgent exit. A group of about 70 remained, many weeping and looking around at their potential assassins only to be stirred again by the leader's next phrase. 'In three minutes time any Christian left in this building will be shot.' Again two more soldiers loaded their guns. More left, some tugging their spouses pleading for them to leave. Numbers were successful, others left in tears having been given reassuring hugs and sent out crying by their solemn partners.

Two elderly women began to pray as silence fell again upon the remaining group of about 30. The young priest sat down on the front row knowing that verbal protest was useless. His natural fear had screamed loudly to leave, but his commitment to Christ that had stood firm and secure in difficult times, knew this was his place on this particular Sabbath. He had heard of similar stories of pastors and church members that had dis-appeared or been murdered in cold blood because of their religious conviction. He knew of many others who had gone 'too far' in the eyes of the 'party' and were now wasting away in Siberian labour camps. He had not really thought this would ever happen to him. Now that he stared death in the face he knew there was nowhere to go. It was for this he had lived and for this he would now die.

The leader spoke again. 'In one minute any Christian left in this building will be shot.' No one moved, the decision was made and the fearful few remained exchanging glances of anxiety and encouragement. The seconds ticked past in an agonising eternity; no one moved as the door was slammed shut. The leader nodded his head at which point it appeared every gun was being loaded up to unleash its deadly chambers, but as they did the soldiers began to lower their guns to the floor and all their eyes turned to the spokesman at the front.

'My apologies for the crudeness of our methods' he said, with a husky but warm voice. *'Actually we don't want to shoot anybody today. We just wanted to talk to a Christian who could tell us about the Jesus whom you follow and we wanted to make sure we heard it from the genuine article!'*

In a Movement destined to be permanently at war until Christ returns, it needs to be filled with 'genuine articles'. This book will seek in part to define what such 'an article' might look like.

Chapter 1

Victories Past

What they did and the legacy they left

Once Upon a Time

The Salvation Army is a metaphor of living doctrine. The war of salvation still rages between the powers of darkness and the people of the kingdom. For those within The Salvation Army this is a call to arms, to lay hold of your biblical and organisational inheritance, to take ownership of that which through a life of obedience is rightfully yours. For those not within it much of the same still applies, there is only one salvation war and only one true **salvation** army, which is the Body of Christ. This book provides a glimpse of what once was, and seeks to hold out the possibilities of a glorious future.

The heritage of The Salvation Army is indeed a proud one, and it is essential to understand the key foundations upon which it is built if we are to correctly focus ourselves today. In our days of quick fix maintenance and quick fix thrills we can easily fall prey to this particular spirit of immediacy within our culture. We could be fooled into thinking that all we need is to rediscover some slick idea that Booth used and it will all be okay. Nothing could be further from the truth. An honest look at our history will reveal that the primary driving force behind our success was not so much innovation or creativity but, as Col Philip

Needham suggests, the Booth's actual understanding of the gospel.

Barring a few glorious exceptions, Christianity in the 1860s had largely become a middle-class pastime with 90% of the working-class totally untouched or reached by the gospel. It was in this context that Booth and his workers began to re-evaluate what the gospel was really all about, and in this context they came up with the following principles.

Universality

They came to realise that the cultural entrapment of the gospel for the 'Who can afford it' middle classes, with their horrid practice of pew rental, was not the true gospel for the *'Whosoever . . . . '* They took Jesus seriously when he said that *'God so loved the world that he gave his only Son,'* meaning that anything other than universal accessibility to the gospel was an undoubted and offensive heresy. Jesus did not say 'For God so loved the Church . . . ,' assuming the primary focus of Jesus' death and resurrection was for some religious elite. No, the gospel was not the gospel unless it was available both geographically and culturally to all people.

God was a missionary God who was into the business of 'seeking and saving' the lost and the church was to replicate that same heart. That was what Jesus had commanded in the Great Commission (Matthew 28:19–20), that all 'tribes' (ethnic groups) should have a chance to hear the gospel, irrespective of race, creed or social class.

> *'Therefore go and make disciples of all nations, baptising them in the name of the Father and of the Son and of the Holy Spirit, and teaching them to obey everything I have commanded you. And surely I am with you always, to the very end of the age.'* (Matthew 28:19–20)

This universal gospel was generally not being preached

and so The Salvation Army in characteristic, if not arrogant, fashion, set out to save the world. 'Every land is my fatherland...'[1] stated Bramwell Booth, William's son and successor, 'for all lands belong to my heavenly Father.' Consequently all of them needed to hear the gospel. The task of reaching this world for Christ was the only rationale for the Army's existence '...all those who are on the Lord's side should aim at this great and godlike purpose and direct and devote all their energies to its accomplishment' was William's comment on the matter of world mission. The gospel **was** the gospel for the whosoever and no compromise to this could be permitted.

For many religious types 'common folk' being in church was quite repulsive. They didn't talk right, act right, dress right or even smell right. Booth had discovered this unholy bigotry in his early days of evangelism. The young idealist naively took street people into elitist, cold and uncaring churches, only for them to be ejected by the 'decent' folk. This conditional access to the gospel was nothing new but was exactly what Jesus had encountered in the Temple (Mark 11:15–17). This particular area of the Temple building was the only place that a Gentile could go and encounter God; yet, as we see, the cultural, economic and religious institutions barred any access to them. Jesus challenged this 1st century heresy and commentators see this as the key turning point in the fatal opposition that Jesus faced as he challenged these powerful institutions. As they opposed Christ, so they opposed Booth, who began his crusade to ensure everybody had a chance to hear and encounter the life-transforming message of Jesus. Nothing short of this truly reflected the universal gospel, hence nothing less would be preached and lived by the early Army.

In military terms they did not see themselves as defenders of some religious enclave from which they occasionally fired artillery and launched 'hit and run' commando raids only to return to their 'safe haven' citadels. No, this was an all-out offensive into enemy territory where the majority of lost people were to be found. The greatest form of 'limited accessibility' to the gospel is when those trusted with its communication refuse to move out from the safety of their own turf. 'If people want to hear they must come to where we are' was the unspoken but strongly held attitude. On our terms, in our way, within our culture and buildings was the normative context for encountering God. This was not good enough for Jesus at the Temple and consequently could not be for the early Salvationists.

Catherine Booth, William's wife and partner in the gospel, was to comment precisely on this issue.

> 'If they will not come inside our consecrated buildings, we must get them in their unconsecrated ones, or out under the canopy of heaven.'[2]

There was no place they would not go to make the gospel available to those who so desperately needed it, but who would rarely if ever get a chance to hear it, because of the prejudiced church culture of their day. Catherine continued:

> 'Do not build churches and wait for people to come to you but *"go ye"* – run after them, seek them out and *"preach My gospel to every creature."* Thrust yourself and your message on the attention of men.'[3]

Whether it was culture, prejudice, perverted theology or opposition, nothing was to stop this universal gospel getting out.

The early Salvationists understood that the gospel was never culture-free. It always had to be communicated out of one culture and translated into a form that could be understood by another. Booth commented 'We must capture the need and spirit of the day, transform it and use what it offers to bring the message of Jesus to all people.' They sought to follow the biblical example of the *'men of Issachar who understood the times and knew what*

Israel should do' (1 Chronicles 12:32), and the New Testament incarnational principle of cultural engagement so clearly demonstrated by Paul in Athens (Acts 17:22–28). This essential dynamic was the one first described by C.H. Spurgeon who suggested that they held the gospel in one hand and a newspaper in the other. Then they sought to bring the two together.

Booth-Tucker, an early Army missionary in India, took this very seriously. As Jesus had *'become one flesh and dwelt among mankind'* (John 1:14), so he tried hard to identify with those he sought to reach. Adopting their dress and lifestyle, it was noted by the *India Mirror* of Calcutta:

> 'If The Salvation Army can prove that Christianity really is the religion of the poor ... by putting on the mendicant's ochre garb, that it can dance, shout and march with the ordinary proletarian poor ... It will have done enough service towards the future evangelisation of India.'[4]

Nothing, not even a missionary's inherent culture, was to stop this universal gospel being universally accessible to the 'whosoever'.

Sacrifice

Although Army martyrs were thankfully few, they were significant and were an honest reflection of the spirit of sacrifice that abounded in the early days. There literally was no mountain too high, no river too deep nor any sacrifice too costly for this radical army of Holy Ghost terrorists. Booth set the tone by his life and words:

> 'Men and women who will die at their post are the very sort in demand just now in The Salvation Army and elsewhere. They are what the world needs, what we are praying for and what God wants.'[5]

This almost insane extremism was the hallmark of our Movement and it was this that attracted so many from the established church to rally around Booth's banner.

Whether it was facing abuse in the open air, ridicule from family and friends, selling all their possessions for the poor or starving themselves as an act of self-denial, the early Salvationists did anything in order to get the job done. The existence of the bonnet is evidence enough of the kinds of sacrifice made. As bricks, stones and rotten vegetables were thrown, the head needed to be protected. The other option was to not witness in the open air lest someone get hurt, but few would have dared to suggest such a possibility, so the black tar and straw crash hat was invented and adorned (see Endnote p. 39). Booth preached and lived an uncompromising life of devotion and sacrifice:

> 'This consecration involves the giving up of pleasures and satisfaction ... it involves a life of self-denial and toil ... offering ourselves to live and suffer for the salvation of the world.'[6]

Lunn tells the story in *Salvation Dynasty* of the efforts of Booth Tucker at bringing the gospel to a particular village, only to be rejected by them. Later that day Tucker and his companion were asleep under a tree. When villagers saw the swollen and cut feet on the bare-footed Westerner, their hearts were moved and they invited them back to share more of Christ. Tucker was later to comment that he had preached his best sermon whilst asleep. This culture of sacrifice was emulated around the army world. The young pioneers in Worthing, England, stood firm in the face of violent opposition from the skeleton Army. The brutality and abuse they received only served to add to their commitment to witness in the open air; the greater the opposition the greater the commitment to sacrifice. Whether it was Tucker's heroics in India or the corporate Army witness in Worthing in the face of violent opposition, the cost was counted and paid.

Many were scarred in the salvation war and wore these scars like medals. This was just part of the expected norm for a soldier in this war. 'No pain, no gain' was the maxim and the Booths drove their soldiers on to live lives of uncompromising sacrifice, for they knew nothing else would get the job done. Catherine said,

> 'Show the world a real, living, self-sacrificing, hard-working, toiling, triumphing religion and the world will be influenced by it, but anything less they will turn around and spit upon.'[7]

Even with this call William found himself having to call for balance and less extremism. You could almost hear the troops questioning Booth's level of commitment when of necessity he had to send out a memo banning his officers from starving themselves, such was the atmosphere of sacrifice. This radical sacrifice fertilised the soil of spiritual revolution that was to so firmly establish the phenomenon of The Salvation Army around the world.

Simplicity

Closely linked to this spirit of sacrifice was a strong commitment to a simple lifestyle. This served two purposes, firstly to make more resources available for the task of mission and secondly to live counter-culturally to the heavily materialistic culture in the increasingly con-sumerist society of the day. So much misery, then, as now, was caused by the myth that 'to have is to be happy', that the ever increasing acquisition of wealth and comfort would bring the contentment all hungered for but few attained.

An essential part of the liberation of early Salvationists was freedom from the worship of 'Mammon'. They were free to worship God and obey his call upon their lives in bringing salvation to the world. God's redemptive work-ings in the world could only be discerned by those not trapped within it, they could only set others free from their position of freedom. We often sentimentally think that all Booth's early workers were converted people from the economic and cultural gutter; this is more fantasy than fact. So many of the earliest Salvationists, were middle-class business people, who captured Booth's vision and made the sacrifice of living more simply and entering that joyful freedom and abandon.

There is a story that records Booth weeping into his Bible whilst reading the book of Acts crying 'Do it again Lord, do it again.' This prayer was most powerfully answered in reflecting the liberty of giving recorded in the New Testament church (Acts 2:42–7; 4:32–5). If the *'earth is the Lord's and everything in it'* then all resources were to be stewarded appropriately in supporting the 'war effort'. Separation from the world and its weakening influence was demanded and no quarter given to the rival god known as 'Mammon'. Booth warned:

> 'How can men and women love God, deny themselves, and live for souls while they worship the golden calf, and make gain, not godliness, the great purpose of their lives?'[8]

In addition, simplicity of lifestyle brought a credibility to the gospel in the eyes of working-class people who had dismissed the Church as an irrelevant and uncaring vehicle of the oppressive establishment. Christians often ignored the gospel's call to live lives of justice and righteousness, by ignoring the obvious plight of the needy around them, and consequently they blunted the cutting edge of the message. Far from being seen as part of the answer to their plight the Church was seen as part of their problem, siding as it did with those in power who consistently oppressed the poor. The Army modelled something that was radically different, and proved highly attractive to many with its commitment to aggressive simplicity.

Militancy

The word militancy is used here in terms of an extreme expression of discipleship and salvationism. This was demonstrated not just by the military metaphor but also by the attitude to the task and methods used. The Articles of War showed very clearly how Salvationists viewed the battle for the lives of men and women.

> 'I do here and now, and forever, renounce the world with all its sinful pleasures, companionships, treasures and objects and declare my full determination boldly to show myself a soldier of Jesus Christ in all places and companies, no matter what I may have to suffer, do or lose by so doing.'

This was a bloody battle that truly was a matter of life and death and consequently no methodology was barred provided it was moral and pragmatically worked. The establishment was to comment in a critical article on the Army's methods '...they utterly vulgarise the holiest of things.' What they meant by 'holy' was in reality non-biblical, cultural trappings that had been wrapped around the gospel and given almost scriptural authority. The Army sought to peel these layers of non-essentials away to expose the heart of the real thing.

Booth was a pragmatist:

> 'Beginning as I did, with a clean sheet of paper, wedded to no plan ... willing to take a leaf out of anybody's book ... above all, to obey the direction of the Holy Spirit. We tried various methods and those that did not answer we unhesitatingly threw overboard and adopted something else.'

Catherine Booth was to lambast the establishment for its lifting of religious man-made traditions to almost biblical status:

'People contend that we must have quiet, proper, decorous services. I say, **where is your authority for this?**'

Almost nothing was considered untouchable in church structures. It was the mission of the Church to preach Christ that was the only bench mark, everything else was up for grabs. Church traditions were trampled upon if they in any way inhibited the effective communication of the gospel. To suggest anything else was nonsense, if not heresy and idolatry.

The intensity of this perspective opened the doors for the most extreme and at times bizarre kinds of service and outreach, including women wearing night-dresses in the street over their uniforms, or preaching seated backwards on a horse. Even the previously untouchable 'hymnals' were to be mercilessly laid aside for contemporary songs from the dance halls and bars. 'Why should the devil have all the good music?' is the famous quote from Booth, who had no idea he would be quoted so widely, but purely sought to make the gospel available in a music genre that was accessible to those they sought to reach. They would do almost anything to win this war. There was no Geneva Convention in this battle, they were fighting a merciless foe who 'took no prisoners' and consequently their single-minded militancy was necessary to reach those untouched by the gospel of Jesus Christ.

Passion

This was what beat in the heart of the early Army. An insatiable passion for Jesus and consequently an aching passion for the lost. Pumping through the veins of all our early endeavours was this condition of the heart and mind. In prayer, worship, preaching and mercy ministry this passion was the hallmark. Even if you did not know where an Army meeting was, you could normally hear it and sense its spirit-empowered energy in and around the events. Its sheer passion attracted your attention and drew thousands to hear the message.

Booth described this intensity:

> 'Salvationists despise cold formalism and love red-hot religion.'

This was no overstatement. Current-day debate regarding the Holy Spirit and his manifestations would have been laughed at as the early Salvationists hungered and thirsted after all they could get of God, and when they prayed 'Send the fire' they meant it! This was not some sentimental, doctrinal creed flavoured with religious political correctness, but rather an urgent cry from their hearts. They came expectant to meet with God and would not leave until they had. Their meetings were marked by a brokenness and humility before an awesome and gracious God, whom they expected would hear and answer their prayers. Supernatural manifestations of God's Spirit were sought after and expected, which only added to the individual and corporate passion they experienced and expressed.

Bramwell Booth records such an event at their six-monthly Council of War in 1878.

> 'At night Corbridge led a hallelujah meeting till 10 o'clock. Then we commenced an All-Night of Prayer. Two hundred and fifty people were present till 1 am; two hundred or so after. A tremendous time. From the very first Jehovah was passing by, searching, softening, and subduing every heart. The power of the Holy Ghost fell on Robinson and prostrated him. He nearly fainted twice. The brother of the Blandys entered into full liberty, and then he shouted, wept, clapped his hands, danced, amid a scene of the most glorious and heavenly enthusiasm. Others meanwhile were lying prostrate on the floor, some of them groaning aloud for perfect deliverance ... it was a blessed night.'[9]

Booth overtly encouraged this experiential theology:

> 'God does not confine himself to sending messages to men through his people, or through books, but he himself, goes straight to people's hearts and so influences them as to make them feel what he wants them to do.' [10]

They sang passionately and earnestly 'Give us the promised Holy Ghost, we want another Pentecost', such was their desire to meet and encounter the living God. It was not for some navel-gazing experience but rather empowerment for mission: 'To make our weak hearts strong and brave ... to live a dying world to save – **send the fire!**' It was this passion that set them apart from the established churches and which drew thousands to the early meetings. Again Booth comments on this contagious, spirit empowered magnetism that was the fruit of what he called 'Pentecostal baptism'.

> 'How much more might be done if you all had received this Pentecostal baptism in all its fullness? If every soul were inflamed, and every lip touched and every mind illuminated, and every heart purified with hallowed flame? ... The whole city would feel it. God's people in every direction would catch fire, and the sinners would fly on every side. Difficulties would vanish, devils be conquered, infidels believe, and the glory of God be displayed. As it is written, every valley would be filled, and every mountain and will be bought low, and the crooked path would be made straight, and the rough ways be made smooth, and all flesh would see the salvation of God.'

Passion, grounded in the reality of God's Spirit and the hunger of his people, drove the Army forward.

Transformation

Charles Dickens, writing at the time, is merciless in his attack on the Christians who did not act on the intrinsic connection between the gospel and their poverty ridden environment. In his greatest satire, *Bleak House*, the young beggar Jo dies by the roadside, utterly neglected by an uncaring society. The author's moral outrage breaks through the literary convention of the third person as for the first time Dickens turns personally to address his audience:

> 'Dead your majesty. Dead, my Lords and gentlemen. Dead, Right Reverends and Wrong Reverends of every order. Dead, men and women born with Heavenly compassion in your hearts. And dying thus around us every day.'[11]

It was the transformation of this horrendously unjust world that The Salvation Army was to turn its attention to. Whether it was by the simple act of giving a hot drink to the homeless or the mammoth achievements of establishing labour exchanges, improving working conditions in the match factories or helping to outlaw child prostitution, the Army sought to model something different. Paul's statement that *'If anyone is in Christ, he is a new creation; the old has gone, the new has come'* (2 Corinthians 5:17), was taken as foundational. It spoke of radical change in the life of a new believer.

Tragically, the common religious habit of separating the sacred and the secular dominated much religious thinking. Assuming that spiritual reality and living in the physical world were separate issues, an assumption still very much alive and kicking in our own day, this philosophy destroyed the heart of true spirituality to leave people guessing as to the nature of what change, if any, had taken place. The supposed 'new creation' became a remoulding of spiritual compromise which at most changed people's geography on a Sunday morning but left their heart, mind and will unchanged.

The Army sought to preach and live the life of transformed holiness as the process of sanctification took place. Catherine stated:

> 'We are told over and over again that God wants his people to be pure, and that purity in their hearts is the very central idea and end and purpose of the gospel of Jesus Christ.'[12]

Every aspect of character and lifestyle was to be transformed as it was surrendered to the lordship of Christ. No part of life was to be left untouched by this transforming power of the gospel and energising of the Holy Spirit. Family and business life, relationships, morality, finance, education and romance; literally everything was under the spotlight of renewal, as God got hold of people's lives. It was evidence of this kind of transformation with lifestyles changed beyond recognition, that spoke of the effectiveness and character of this charismatic movement known as The Salvation Army. This was no empty piety, but powerful revolutions of lives and consequently communities.

> 'We are a Salvation people, this is our speciality: getting saved, keeping saved and getting others saved...'

Booth was very clear as to our key priority and function. The Army stood in the evangelical tradition of their Wesleyan roots, that a commitment to Christ was an individual decision of the heart and mind to follow. This was not dependent upon any religious or sacramental practice but a declaration of repentance in response to the undeserving love and grace of God. Classic hymns like 'Amazing Grace' and 'O happy day' celebrated the wonderful day when Jesus washed their sins away. Outward forms and practices were merely a physical demonstration of an inward revolution that had taken place. This 'about turn' of repentance was to kick-start a process of transformation that was to affect every aspect of life.

The whole gospel

Booth's *Darkest England and the Way Out* caused offence within both the religious and political establishment. A 'man of the cloth' getting involved in political and economic life was a scandal and most rare, bar a few glorious exceptions. Yet for the Army it made absolute sense in respect to the 'whole' gospel bringing transformation to the 'whole' of a person's life.

A contemporary of Booth's was to comment:

> 'The Darkest England scheme is but an outward embodiment and manifestation of Him who died and rose again in the carrying out of that grand scheme. The Spirit of the Lord was upon Him ... that Spirit has now arisen in England and is present in the Darkest England scheme of The Salvation Army ... the Spirit of Jesus Christ now walks the streets of London and those of our great cities; is present in the slums, the shelters, the elevators; speaks peace to the converts at their lowly meetings, and gives sight to many who are blind among the poor, needy and suffering.'[13]

It was nonsense merely to seek spiritual transformation whilst ignoring all those other aspects of a person's life that were in need of salvation and change. This was an essential part of the gospel mandate to redeem not only lives but cultures, socio-political systems, economics and anywhere else where evil and injustice reigned. This was to be for the Army one of its most powerful and influential contributions as many of those things challenged, changed, and impacted many nations around the world, irrespective of unpopularity, opposition or cost. Whether it was establishing labour exchanges, or challenging the evils of child prostitution the Army sought to present the 'whole' gospel to the 'whole' world.

Christ came to save people, not just their souls. With the introduction of the Cab-horse Charter, Booth sought to change the plight of the three million people of darkest England. This was no shallow 'welfare handout', but more a focus on long-term change in people's lives, rescuing them from the great twin evils of destitution and despair.

Roger Green comments on the emerging 'dual mission' of The Salvation Army:

> 'Hitherto the Army's chief concern had been for personal salvation from sin, and social concerns were secondary, but increasing in importance. Now, however, the movement was engaged in two works; personal salvation and social salvation; it now had a dual mission.'[14]

Booth criticised the established churches for failing to redress these broader social concerns:

> 'Why all this apparatus of temples and meeting houses to save men from perdition in a world which is to come, while never a helping hand is stretched out to save them from the inferno of their present life?'[15]

For Booth this was not so much a new theology of salvation but rather a very broadened one in which those things he had been preaching for years took on a whole new dimension:

> 'But with this discovery there also came another which has been growing in clearness and intensity from that hour to this; which was that I had two gospels of deliverance to preach – one for each world, or rather, one gospel which applied alike to both. I saw that when the Bible said *"he that believeth shall be saved,"* it meant not only saved from the miseries of the future

world but from the miseries of this also. That it came with the promise of salvation here and now; from hell and sin and vice and crime and idleness and extravagance, and consequently very largely from poverty and disease and the majority of kindred foes.'[16]

This developed a new, pragmatic, and theological dynamism within the movement that was to map so much of its future impact upon the world.

Institutional transformation

However, it was not just society that they sought to see transformed, but also the church traditions themselves. Contemporary perspectives upon leadership were challenged on many fronts. The early Army ignored the tendency of other churches not to put young people in leadership positions, with large numbers of their officers and workers being in their late teens and early twenties. Even more controversial was the Army's view on women's ministry and their role in leadership. Booth was very clear on the issue; having seen his wife, daughters and granddaughters give valiant service in leadership, he wrote in his message to soldiers:

> 'First and foremost, I insist on the equality of woman with man. Every officer and soldier should insist upon the truth that woman is as important, as valuable, as capable, and as necessary to the progress and happiness of the world as man ... To many men, woman is little more than a plaything ... a piece of property, a slave in everything but name, oftimes being treated with less consideration than the horses that run in the omnibus, or the beasts that are fattening for slaughter. Now, The Salvation Army has done and is doing something to combat these hideous heathen notions.'[17]

His famous quip, 'some of my best men are women' was not a patronising slight but a prophetic statement to a sexist society and Church. Far from being limited to the flower rota, women became many of the Army's frontline troops going to places that few dared to tread. My own wife's grandmother Mrs Commissioner Mitchell, walked 60 miles on her own to her appointment as a young nineteen-year-old in rural India. On the streets, in the slums and in the bars, these warriors of Christ fearlessly proclaimed the gospel, and led the Army forward in its world-wide revolution. The early Army also challenged the historical divide between priesthood and laity, seeing priesthood as the responsibility of everyone. In a letter Booth explained:

> 'The idea never dawned on me that a line was to be drawn between me who had nothing to do but preach, and a saved apprentice lad ... I have lived, thank God, to witness the separation between layman and cleric become more and more obscured, and to see Jesus Christ's idea of changing in a moment ignorant fisherman into fishers of men, nearer and nearer realisation.'[18]

The early Salvationists saw no biblical or pragmatic rationale for a limited, professional priesthood. They aimed, therefore to empower the laity. All vocations were valid, as believers sought to 'flesh out' the gospel in their work place. Furthermore when, very early in our history, a creeping 'professionalising' of the ministry began to take place, Booth was quick to the attack:

> 'Some murmurs have reached us ... as to whether "The Officer" may not defeat its good intentions and cut its own throat by converting officers into preachers. It is rumoured that at some corps the soldiers and sergeants never have a chance except in the open air, the Captain reserving all the indoor meetings to himself. Surely this is an exaggeration. The General is going to deal with this danger. Let us be awake to it, and do our utmost to avoid the snare.'[19]

Victorious

Finally the early Army was carried upon the wings of a victory that was eternally theirs in Christ and merely needed claiming and living in the present. These were no 'superficial triumphalists' as they would be labelled today, but very deep and 'committed' triumphalists. The result was never open to question. Theirs was not a victory to be prayed for or even sought after, but something guaranteed by the resurrection of Christ and sealed by the power of the Spirit.

Their almost suicidal trust in the power and victory of the resurrected Jesus, led them to confront the greatest powers of the day with almost regal arrogance: like Booth-Tucker who in the open air confronted the imperial authorities. Consequently they were arrested but once released were out on the streets preaching again. Such was their sense and theology of the victorious gospel they just did not care. *'If God is for us, who can be against us?'* (Romans 8:31) was their maxim, and this was a very real war.

> 'Here is a war in which you will win celestial honours; honours that will last forever. Will you enlist? We take all recruits in this Army. If you have a heart to love, come along. We want men and women indifferent to all other aims and ends but the extension of the Kingdom of Jesus.'[20]

They feared neither man nor devil. The victory of Christ was all-encompassing over the powers of evil and darkness. This was very much a spiritual battle and spiritual victory which needed declaring and proclaiming so as to dislodge the 'god of this world'.

> 'We cannot bow, or notice, or persuade the devil out of his favourite citadel or stronghold ... there is only one way to drive him out and that is by actual, self-

sacrificing warfare. There is nothing for it but to fight and to fight to the death. Who is willing for this?' [21]

Even in the face of much hardship and difficulty the smell of victory was always in the air. They reflected the 'no retreat, no surrender' mentality of Shadrach, Meshach and Abednego who, facing death at the hands of the tyrant Nebuchadnezzar, still refused to bow to his idolatrous desires no matter what the cost.

> '*O Nebuchadnezzar, we do not need to defend ourselves before you in this matter. If we are thrown into the blazing furnace, the God we serve is able to save us from it … But even if he does not, we want you to know, O king, that we will not serve your gods or worship the image of gold you have set up.*'   (Daniel 3:16–18)

In the war that raged and the battles they fought, they did not even consider defeat a possibility. If God was for them, what did it matter who was against them? They would win through. The consequence of this hardened battle-mentality led to many costly victories that were to brand The Salvation Army onto the religious and cultural heart of the world and provide us, their spiritual offspring, with a rich and glorious heritage as well as a terrifying inheritance.

> 'Fix the anchor of your soul in these glorious proclamations of the Divine will, in these glorious prophetic announcements with which the Book abounds. Plod on patiently, work and struggle; weep and pray on. It will hasten this glorious consummation.' [22]

The World for God

This song of Evangeline Booth expressed the raison d'être for The Salvation Army.

The world for God! The world for God!
There's nothing else will meet the hunger of my
    soul.
I see forsaken children, I see the tears that fall
From women's eyes, once merry, now never laugh
    at all;
I see the sins and sorrows of those who sit in
    darkness;
I see in lands far distant, the hungry and oppressed.
But behold! On a hill, Calvary! Calvary!

The world for God! The world for God!
I give my heart! I'll do my part!
The world for God! The world for God!
I give my heart! I will do my part!

The world for God! The world for God!
I call to arms the soldiers of the blood and fire:
Go with the Holy Bible. Its words are peace and
    life
To multitudes who struggle with crime and want
    and strife.
Go with your songs of mercy, show Christ in loving
    kindness,
Make known the sufferings of the cross, the sacrifice
    of God;
For behold! On a hill, Calvary! Calvary!

The world for God! The world for God!
For this, dear Lord, give to my soul consuming fire.
Give fire that makes men heroes, turns weakness into
    might,
The fire that gives the courage to suffer for the fight,
The fire that changes fearing to pentecostal daring,
The fire that makes me willing for Christ to live or
    die;
For behold! On a hill, Calvary! Calvary! [23]

This clarion call still needs to be at the very epicentre of our movement's soul, but it must be viewed within its new context. The world in which the Booths first uttered these words no longer exists. It has gone forever and has been replaced by something new. A world of many worlds. The global village that we now inhabit is fundamentally distinct from that in which we were born. Warfare, for example, has changed dramatically. The weapons used to fight the Boer War were significantly different from those hi-tech ones used in the Gulf War. The blockbuster film *Independence Day* portrayed the alien invaders as taking only a few days to destroy civilisation (as we know it), with their advanced technology. The reality is that we have the capacity with our weapons of mass destruction, to annihilate ourselves within minutes.

This being so, there are some constants that remain for how battles are lost and won. The training and preparation of soldiers before a battle, their ownership and commitment of the cause for which they are fighting, have been, and will always be essential. If they are not properly established, the fate of a war could change. In many military contexts effective soldiering is preceded by the preparation of 'boot camp'. It is here that the foundations of a good soldier are laid and established. Slothful and destructive habits are laid aside and new ones formed. Those skills, attitudes, character foundations and values needed to create effective fighting machines, are honed and refined. Without confronting bad discipline, cowardice and other weaknesses during boot camp, soldiers go out ill equipped and a risk to others who depend upon them to fulfil their duty effectively. Refresher courses or remedial classes help supplement this initial input, as does more advanced and specialised training. Yet most of the key battles need to be fought and won at boot camp to produce soldiers who win the wars they fight.

This is exactly how it is within the spiritual war in which the Church of God is engaged. If we are to win this world for God there are numerous battles that must be won by the soldiers themselves, within their own lives, as part preparation for effective involvement in the prosecution of the salvation war. If these personal battles are lost, it will make victory in the major battle difficult, if not impossible. We are called to love God with all our *'heart mind and soul'* (will) (Matthew 22:37). This is not a neutral decision, that will leave us unchallenged, but is at the very heart of who we are as soldiers of Jesus Christ, and will consequently be challenged every inch of the way. The rest of this book will outline the nature of the battles in these three areas, and strategies for winning them.

Throughout the text I will use the term warrior instead of soldier, as I lift up the ideal to which we are called. The dictionary describes soldiers as those who relate to the structures and systems of an army, whereas warriors find their identity in relation to the prosecution of the war. We are at war, we need an army of fighting warriors, not parade-ground soldiers.

In the eastern evangelical church, when 'war' was declared with the loading of the guns, a line was drawn to discover the 'genuine articles' of faith. This is the ideal to which we are called.

Endnote

'When cadets assembled in London in May 1880 for the opening of the training home for women officers, so great was the divergence in their headgear, that Mrs Booth then determined to devise something that would be suitable for uniform wear, cheap, strong and large enough to protect the heads of the wearers from cold as well as from brickbats and other missiles.'

(Robert Sandell, *The History of The Salvation Army*, Vol. 2., p. 48. Thomas Nelson & Sons Ltd)

Chapter 2

Battle for the Mind

Thinking as a warrior should think

As the waves crashed around the ship the evil slave trader, this dealer in human flesh, considered his life and all he had done. As the seas rolled with ever-increasing turbulence, so did his mind. A mental storm was beginning to brew. His human cargo, incarcerated below would, as in most trips, arrive with not all still alive. Between the lashing of the waves cries could be heard from the desperate company beneath decks. Through disease, suffocation, and at times starvation, numbers would die and provide the sharks with a mighty feast. None cared too much if some who went over were not actually dead; it only hastened the inevitable.

Brutality was part of the control: beatings, floggings, rapes. They were all too common a part of the socially condoned evil of slavery. Families were devastated, whole communities ripped apart, husband from wife, child from parents. This ebony sea of humanity was violated with inhumane intensity. Flesh and bone were pawned as commodities, exchanged with little or no thought of the injury being suffered in body, mind and spirit. Thought of as somewhat inferior to other men and women, human rights were denied to those who were viewed as less than human. Freedom was stolen in the name of commerce.

Scores had died as a result of man's 'financial investments'. Untold misery had been meted out upon the African peoples and during it all no question of guilt nor disquiet had ever flashed across his mind. Yet this day was different. This day, in the *midst of the life-threatening storm, he suddenly became aware of his own mortality and the fragility of life, causing fear to grip his heart. The arrogance and harshness of his bigotry began to be challenged. What had been the invincible bastion of an emotional vacuum began to crumble. Thoughts of God and sin, not entertained since he was a child, began to travel across his mind. Guilt, considered by him a rare and unnecessary sensation, began to consume him. His heart began to stir as the pages of his life began turning before his eyes.*

None will ever know the full story of what took place during that treacherous night. A revolution of mind and heart had begun that would have life-transforming consequences. More than canvas and wood were thrown into turmoil that night. A battle had begun for how this man viewed God, himself and the sanctity of life itself. Decisions needed to be made, attitudes had to be changed, a mind had to be renewed. It was this man who, as a result of the considerations begun that night, eventually bowed his knee before Jesus and became a champion of the powerless slaves. One day, when thinking back to this mental and spiritual journey, he penned the words that have brought challenge and hope to millions:

> Amazing Grace how sweet the sound,
> That saved a wretch like me,
> I once was lost but now am found,
> Was blind but now I see.[24]

John Newton had won the battle for his mind.

An Age-Old Challenge

The battle for our minds, which determines so many of our actions, is the first area of conflict that we will consider in the creation of a warrior. It is an issue at the very heart of who we are as people.

The interior design of our minds has been modelled and shaped by many different influences. Our family, education, culture and experience have all contributed to how it looks on the inside and how reality is perceived on the outside. This interior design is highly influential upon our effectiveness in the war. The design is not permanent; when we become a Christian, a transformation and 're-design' begins to take place. Our own influence upon what that new-look mind is like is significant, and is largely determined by the choices we make. Our salvation is a gift of grace, our only involvement being our grateful accept-ance. Yet the changing shape and look of our minds is very much a battle in which we are personally engaged, and it must be won by us.

In writing to the Roman church, the apostle Paul makes it absolutely clear that when we become a Christian, a revolution of the mind as well as the spirit needs to take place.

> '*Therefore, I urge you, brothers, in view of God's mercy, to offer your bodies as living sacrifices, holy and pleasing to God – this is your spiritual act of worship. Do not conform any longer to the pattern of this world, but be transformed by the renewing of your mind. Then you will be able to test and approve what God's will is – his good, pleasing and perfect will.*'
> (Romans 12:1–2)

In the light of this passage, we need to be aware of the following:

1. Paul was writing to people who had only recently become Christians. His aim was to move them beyond 'first steps' Christianity into greater maturity and effectiveness. The whole passage is a reminder of the key point that 'Christians are born and disciples are made.' The conversion of an individual is not the **end** of a journey but the **beginning**.
2. There is a way of living to 'the pattern of this world' that these Christians were still modelling. Whether it be overt habits of rebellion against God's revealed will or the 'anti-God' values that are unconsciously owned

in most cultures, this an ever-present problem for the Christian seeking to be 'in the world, but not of it.'

3. It is only whilst the necessary **process** of transformation takes place that God's perfect will can be discerned and worked out in an individual's life. Until that point we can continue only to live a Christianised version of the world's values and lifestyles. This process is necessary to get the 'world out of us' so God can trust us and send us 'out into the world.'

The battle faced by the Roman church is one for the **mind**. It is an on-going struggle which the contemporary warrior must also face. In respect of this fact I offer the following as strategies for winning this individual battle.

What Do You See?

The success of the Western children's character 'Thomas the Tank Engine' was quite unexpected and incredible in Japan. Advertisers were astounded at the way in which a wholly Western, dubbed-over product, took off in such a diverse eastern context. With customary fashion the marketing machine began to ask what other similar products could possibly be launched with a similar degree of success. It didn't take long for them to pick up the potential of launching 'Postman Pat', as another children's puppet character. The wheels of the advertising world moved into motion and significant amounts of money were poured into launching this new product. No doubt images of further share price increases and personal bonuses, filled the minds of those involved. It was another amazing opportunity to maximise this new and incredibly lucrative market.

The launch date came, the shops were stacked, they opened – and it was a sales disaster. Nowhere near the numbers expected were sold, much money was lost. When they discovered the reason, it was a surprise to all concerned, and helps us consider this important issue. Postman Pat has only three fingers, and the only people in Japanese culture who have three fingers are triad gang members, who sever their little fingers as a symbol of their gang membership. Parents obviously didn't want their kids playing with puppets that represented the scourge of Japanese society. No one had asked the right questions. The advertisers had not seen, and consequently had not thought, what their prospective customers had thought. The issue of what reality is perceived within the mind, is not a new one.

Elisha was an enemy army's nightmare. Every time they went to make a specific move, he would prophesy what was going to happen, spoiling the element of surprise and bringing victory to the Israelites. So a focused attack was made to deal with this military prophet. His location was identified and a significant force sent to deal with this irritant.

The servant of Elisha awoke to a frightening world as he looked through his 'own' glasses of understanding and saw these opposing forces come to destroy his master and him. However, when replaced with a whole new pair he experienced a transformed revelation (2 Kings 6:15–17). This teaches us an important lesson in the process of renewing our mind: we all wear glasses. They have been shaped and moulded by the culture in which we live, our family background and our experience of life. They radically affect the way we live and consequently the kind of disciples we become.

World-view

The technical term for these glasses of understanding is 'world-view' – that through which we view the world and the framework into which all things must find their place of acceptance or rejection. For the Romans whom Paul was writing to in the passage quoted earlier, 'humility' would have been seen very negatively. The supremacy and un-rivalled power of the Roman empire was proudly held dear. Yet to followers of Christ, who like the Philipians were called to 'have the same attitude as that of Christ Jesus . . .

who humbled himself,' this aspect of their world-view was challenged and the gospel demanded change. Then, as now, many values and beliefs, held as normal within our world-view, are not necessarily within God's *'perfect and pleasing will.'*

Donald Kraybill in his powerful book *The Upside Down Kingdom* highlights this important fact, showing how so often the values of our culture are in opposition to the gospel.

> 'Kingdom action takes place in the middle of the societal ball park. Kingdom players follow new rules. They listen to another coach. Kingdom values challenge the patterns of social life taken for granted in modern culture. Kingdom habits don't mesh smoothly with dominant cultural trends. They may, in fact, look foolish.' [25]

They provide a lens through which we view reality. I remember as a child eating toffees, wrapped in yellow 'see-through' plastic wrapping. As I chewed I would peer through the paper and reality would take on a whole new perspective. Life took on a lovely yellow glow! Tragically this 'glow of unreality' is sometimes much more than a childhood game.

> 'Often people fail to recognise the extent to which their own lives have been secularised and their churches captivated by the pagan values of the dominant culture ... this group is almost totally unaware of its captivity ... even though many of us have come to vital faith in Christ and our spiritual condition has been changed, too often our values have not altered ... In becoming Christians it appears that many of us have unquestionably attempted to layer our faith right over the top of the secular values with which we have been raised.' [26]

Kraybill continues in similar vein:

> 'The values, beliefs and norms of our society become so deeply ingrained in our mind that we no longer see the alternatives. Throughout the gospels, Jesus presents the Kingdom as a new order breaking in on old ways, old values, old assumptions. If it does anything, the Kingdom of God shatters the assumptions which govern our lives. As Kingdom citizens we can't assume that things are right just because "that's the way they are." The upside down perspective focuses the points of divergence and conflict between God's Kingdom and the Kingdoms of the world.' [27]

Jim Wallis, founder of the Sojourners Community in the ghettos of Washington, takes this analysis one step further, allowing biblical imagery to assess the contemporary scene.

> 'Church historians may someday describe our period as the "American Captivity of the Church." It is no less real than the Babylonian Captivity of the nation of Israel. Our churches are captivated by the values of the secular culture and, for the most part, don't know it.' [28]

The captivity and shaping of a warrior's mind has always been the key to winning battles. The use of psychological propaganda or even torture is evidence enough of this. Still today, evil dictatorships will seek to control minds through indoctrination, ensuring obedience and suppressing opposition.

In terms of the Army of God I feel that our greatest challenge is not from full frontal assault, although that is increasing in intensity, but rather, as Wallis describes, something more insidious and subtle. The corruption and violation of a warrior's mind, is meted out with almost unrivalled force due to the unconscious way that this battle is conducted. Those inherent values and beliefs that have been assimilated into our Christian world-view, slowly but surely destroy our vitality and cutting edge within the war, the impact at times being terminal.

Generations ago 'slavery' was part of the accepted status quo. It was a given fact and for most Christians, many of whom would actually own them, it was not an issue that ever interfaced with their faith. Yet to us contemporary believers the idea of it seems incredible and highly offensive. How could they have been so blind? Yet lest we judge too quickly those for whom 'slavery' was an accepted part of their 'normal' life, Bishop Leslie Newbiggin presents a stinging challenge:

> 'Just as we contemporary Christians look back and wonder how on earth our believing forebears could have condoned and accepted slavery, so future generations will look back to us and wonder how we did the same with the evil of materialism.'

We are told that to boil a toad is relatively easy, provided that you increase the temperature a little bit at a time. The toad will adapt to its compromised and dangerous environment as the heat increases, never realising the terminal potential of its assimilation to its context. So too the warriors who are not aware of the dangers and issues at stake, can find themselves assimilating the predominant values of the anti-God culture around us, destroying and nullifying our impact upon the war.

The actual recognition of the existence of such a battle is one of the most important dynamics in this conflict. Understanding and appreciating our world view and how it influences our actions is an essential aspect of engaging in the battle for our minds.

Vertical selfishness or biblical holiness

Before moving to consider what it means to think Christianly, it is important to pause and reflect how we view our faith. Much of what you will read within this book could be viewed as a kind of shallow gospel of works if we hold a perception of faith that has become so common within the evangelical church. Too often we have viewed our faith in terms of what I call 'vertical selfishness'. This is a faith that is two-dimensional – us and God – by understanding our faith in terms of a purely individual relationship with God in isolation to the rest of the world. Yet we need to realise that we only think in such a way because of the heavy influence of western individualism. This has been a culture which starts with the 'I' and then passes everything through that self-centred and individualistic sieve. This is alien to the biblical image of faith and spirituality. Our faith is a Trinitarian faith. It can only be understood in terms of our relationship with God and the world in which God has placed us. From Genesis to Revelation faith is never to be understood nor expressed in isolation to the world in which that faith is to be lived out. This raises a perspective that is important for us to consider. Our relationship with God is intrinsically linked to our relationship with the affairs and concerns of the community of this globe. The moment we isolate one aspect from the other we violate the holistic nature of our faith.

A Trinitarian God created humankind for a Trinitarian relationship. It is not possible to fully appreciate nor understand biblical faith outside of this framework. God raised up Israel and later the New Testament community of faith to be a working model of his society. His call to Israel was always linked with the *'land'* they were to inherit. The disciples were commissioned to go out into the *world*. At no point and in no way does Scripture ever give us a mandate to consider our faith outside of the context of who we are in God and how we live for God within the global community. You cannot have one without the other. To paraphrase James the brother of Jesus, faith without works is not just dead, it's not biblical faith, full stop.

All that follows must be viewed through this understanding of faith, which is at the **heart** of Salvationism. Some have called it spirituality with its sleeves rolled up. This book holds up the understanding that only this kind of faith is a true reflection of biblical holiness, and is an overt rejection of the vertical selfishness so common within the current day Salvation Army and the wider evangelical Church.

Thinking Christianly

What then does it mean to have a Christian's mind and to think Christianly? How do we discern the difference between what is purely culture and what is important for a Christian? For example some churches carry an unspoken belief that it is somehow more spiritual to wear a suit to church than jeans. This is purely a cultural import from an increasingly outdated and formal framework of life. The Army has its own version in measuring one's spiritual commitment, by the smartness of one's uniform and the regularity with which one turns up at Army events. Again a cultural invention that needs to be sifted. I feel a strong argument could be made to show that if someone spends their time exclusively doing 'church' things and never interacting socially with their 'not-yet-Christian' friends, this itself could be a sign of spiritual shallowness and sterility.

Whatever the issue, this value sieve needs to be used to assist in the renewing of our minds. It is often said that Christians are 'too heavenly minded to be of any worldly good.' Yet the exact opposite is often true. At times we are 'too worldly minded to be of any heavenly use.' We have so immersed ourselves within the dominant values, ideals and dreams of our pagan cultures, that there really is very little difference between the thought-patterns and lifestyles which we follow and those pursued by our 'not-yet-Christian' neighbours and friends.

Road to renewal

Having recognised the importance of this issue we must then move on to 'action' that may change our thinking.

Once 'worldly patterns' are identified, they need to be transformed, and it is to this aim that we now turn our attention.

'Diesel, you idiot!'

These were the words that filled my mind as my car began to jolt and stutter about two miles from the petrol station where I had just filled my diesel vehicle with unleaded petrol. The sense of embarrassment and shame was increased tenfold when I realised that not only would my car fail to complete the journey but it would have to go in for repairs, and I may have caused some very expensive long-term damage (I have done this twice!).

So too with our minds. Fill it with the wrong stuff and it won't work properly and may in the long run 'break-down'. The computing world gives us another helpful analogy. There is a computing principle known as GIGO – an acronym standing for 'Garbage In Garbage Out.' It basically means that if you feed rubbish into a computer, then the computer will reply in kind when you press print. The same is found to be true within our own lives. If we fill our minds with destructive rubbish, then that is exactly what we will see manifested within our lives. What we focus on in private will eventually demonstrate itself within the public arena of our lives. As Oscar Wilde wrote 'What one has done in the secret chamber, one has some day to cry aloud from the rooftops.'

It is stated just as well by James the brother of Jesus when talking about how we use our tongues:

> 'Out of the same mouth come praise and cursing. My brothers, this should not be. Can both fresh water and salt water flow from the same spring?' (James 3:10–11)

This applies reasonably consistently across a very broad area of our lives. For example, if we read pornography it will warp our perspective of sexuality, and how we view members of the opposite sex. Ravi Zacharias articulates clearly that when we 'see' such things they sometimes sear our consciences permanently. To my shame I surrendered at times to the teenage desire for titillation and read and watched some pornography. I remember well the images that went before me. Their power has gone, but the record that remains is somewhat more permanent.

If we fill our minds with the empty dreams and myths of Hollywood's glamour life à la *Vogue* and *Hello* magazines, we will spend our money, set our priorities and map the direction of our lives accordingly. I have talked honestly and candidly with Christian brothers and sisters about the pressure in their efforts to 'keep up' with the yuppie lifestyle of others within their fellowship: a competition driven by secular marketing ploys designed to make us dissatisfied with who we are, with the values of the Kingdom nowhere in sight. A great tragedy is the number of Salvation Army corps who play the same idolatrous games, maybe not with clothes, for navy serge is navy serge, but with cars, houses and holidays.

If we constantly fantasise over romantic encounters, we will make life choices accordingly. If we succumb to the comfort orientation that the majority of advertising seeks to encourage, we will become slothful and lazy regarding the sacrificial demands of the war. The list could go on and we will address some of these issues later on. Suffice to say, what we allow in private will inevitably work out in public.

Changing these things, seeing them renewed from the 'pattern of the world,' demands a great deal of effort and focus, but once done enables us to travel lighter and more efficiently. A helpful analogy may be the launching of a space rocket. The amount of energy needed to escape the initial gravitational pull of the planet far exceeds that needed to travel the hundreds of thousands of miles that follow on its destination. Values and habits have an incredible gravitational pull that sometimes needs significant effort to change. Once achieved, however, vast distances can be travelled with much less effort. I want to suggest the following as ways of escaping this gravitational pull.

Feed It!

It doesn't take a genius to work out who has fed themselves on a healthy, high-fibre, low-fat diet, compared to those of us who have lived on a consistent and balanced diet of chocolate éclairs, fries and burgers. What we feed on often determines what shape we end up with, and how we live. When Jesus stated that *'Man does not live on bread alone but by every word that proceeds from the mouth of God'* (Matthew 4:4), he was lifting up our first important principle, feeding on the Word of God.

God has revealed himself in his word. It is given as an instrument of guidance, inspiration, correction and revelation of the ways and will of God.

> *'All Scripture is God-breathed and is useful for teaching, rebuking, correcting and training in righteousness, so that the man of God may be thoroughly equipped for every good work.'* (2 Timothy 3:16–17)

Brought into our parlance, the Bible is **the** training manual for serious warriors.

The Salvation Army doctrines state:

> 'We believe that the Scriptures of the Old and New Testaments were given by inspiration of God; and that they only constitute the divine rule of Christian faith and practice.'[29]

Yet the tacit affirmation of a creed is one thing; applying it in everyday life is another. I am a struggler in this area. In my better moments I love the word of God; it excites, challenges, motivates and comforts me. In my less 'focused' moments I would rather watch TV, with its sometimes mind-numbing stimulation. Yet my own weakness cannot be allowed to excuse me. This is an issue of discipline and self-control. If we do not feed on the right things we will be 'emaciated warriors', at the mercy of any 'strong thought' that comes along.

We must discipline ourselves to win this battle. At times I am amazed at the high level of theological and biblical illiteracy amongst many of our soldiers and even some officers. Is it any wonder that the world ridicules us for our belief, when our only line of defence turns out to be: 'You ask me how I know he lives? He lives within my heart.' Without denying the validity of this statement, it is a vastly inadequate argument to put before a world which already assumes Christianity to be intellectually bankrupt. We must work hard at knowing **why** we believe what we do.

It is revealing that when many Christians, are faced with a Jehovah's Witness or similar, they feel intimidated. I think this is for two reasons. Firstly, their commitment is unquestionable and puts many of us to shame. As someone once said 'Jehovah's Witnesses are wholly committed to half the truth whereas many evangelical Christians are half committed to the whole truth.' Secondly, we fear their greater knowledge of 'the handbook of war,' the Bible and associated theological issues. Right or wrong, they know their beliefs better than many so-called 'believers.'

Truly, Scripture must become *'a lamp to my feet and a light for my path'* (Psalm 119:105). It can only do this if the mind is continually soaked in its truth and concepts. The only way to have our minds set *'on things above, not on earthly things'* (Colossians 3:2), is to be consumed with the 'word' from above. Through study, reflection, meditation and discussion, we must wrestle with the revelation of God and how it relates to the increasingly complex world in which we live. This is not about throwing Bible verses at everything and everyone, hoping for some kind of easy answer to all of life's challenges. No, it is about feeding on it so that our values, ethics and principles which provide the foundation of our lives are shaped by it, thus enabling us to live distinctive warrior lifestyles.

By this God says:

> *'I will put my law in their minds and write it on their hearts. I will be their God, and they will be my people.'*
> (Jeremiah 31:33)

The meaning of this passage is clear. Our identity, and subsequently our effectiveness as the Army of God, is intrinsically linked to his word shaping our minds. It is a weapon that Jesus used in battling the devil in the desert, and one which Paul encourages us to use along with the rest of the armour of God:

> *'Take ... the sword of the Spirit, which is the word of God.'*
> (Ephesians 6:17)

This is something that we must know, if we are going to use it.

Priorities

I have often heard a dialogue in Army circles about which is more important to have in a corps programme; a Bible study or band practice. Without wishing to belittle the real issues behind this statement, the argument is nonsense. It is like comparing playing a brass instrument and breathing itself. Breath is used to produce music, without it we have no sound. Stop breathing, you have no life. Banding is a valid form of ministry that believers 'do', whereas Bible study is the very lifeblood of who a believer is. Without banding or any other form of ministry we will carry on and do something else, without feeding on God's word we will die.

In addition, we should consume the works of other writers, like biographies of heroes of the faith. These publications call us on in our commitment and stretch our thinking in terms of discipleship, applying biblical truth and understanding how best we might live out our warrior life. So much of my early development as a Christian was influenced by the writings of people like David Watson and Colin Urquhart. More recently, Jim Wallis, Tom Sine, Keith Green, and of course, William and Catherine Booth, have been of great inspiration.

Feed on good food, not on junk.

Preaching to ourselves

It is difficult to express how important this is for the effectiveness of our witness. How and when we feed on God's word isn't so much the issue, just that we do feed on it. This is to help us communicate to others as well as guarding ourselves from wrong thinking. The story is told of the young boy who sat looking out of his window, and noticed a street preacher standing on a wooden box preaching to an assembled crowd. Every day the man would stand there proclaiming his message. After a while the crowds diminished to a handful of people and eventually none would stop but just walked on by. One day the young boy went out and asked the man as to why he still preached when no one was listening. The man replied, 'Son, when I first came here to speak I did it so that all the people could hear and know, now I do it so that I won't forget.' I mention this not as an encouragement for largely ineffective street communication, but rather as a challenge for us to guard our minds and keep them filled with truth in a world of lies.

I think therefore I am? I think?

It is not only in the area of biblical study that we must wrestle but at a seemingly more basic level of 'thinking' at all. The Salvation Army is known for many things, a faith at work, Christianity with its sleeves rolled up, a group of people with their hearts to God and their hands to man. Yet it would be fair to say that we are not renowned for our incisive thinking, our academic credibility or depth of cerebral authority. This is not to say that we don't have people who think very deeply or are lacking in any ability to engage with the world in this way. Yet perhaps our lack of focus on developing a strong 'thinking culture' has left us, like many of our evangelical brothers and sisters, extremely weak in a very important area of our corporate and individual armoury.

In his book *Fit Bodies Fat Minds* Os Guinness speaks strongly against the perceived trend of anti-intellectualism within the evangelical church:

> 'Anti-intellectualism is a disposition to discount the importance of truth and the life of the mind. Living in a sensuous culture and an increasingly emotional democracy, Western evangelicals in the last generation have simultaneously toned up their bodies and slackened off their minds. The result? Many suffer from a modern form of what the ancient stoics called "mental hedonism" – having fit bodies but fat minds.'[30]

He urges the church to begin 'thinking' again having stopped thinking in preference to this experiential and cultural assimilation. He clearly views this position as a serious issue in the battle for the mind:

> 'At root evangelical anti-intellectualism is both a scandal and a sin. It is a scandal in the sense of being an offence and stumbling block that needlessly hinders serious people from considering the Christian faith and coming to Christ. It is a sin because it is a refusal, contrary to the first of Jesus' two great commandments, to love the Lord our God with our minds.'[31]

My own experience over the last few years has led me to believe that this analysis is not only a fair reflection of much of evangelicalism but also a frightening, even damning assessment of much of our Army culture. Our holiness roots and focus upon experience that has been encapsulated into such a incredibly tight-knit sub-culture has, I fear left us somewhat light in this area and produced a sub-culture of salvationism that struggles to stand its ground when tested philosophically or theologically. This is a situation that must change. The Christian faith is increasingly under tight scrutiny. Many perceive our faith as intellectually bankrupt and void of any real substance. Thankfully this has not been caused by people seriously engaging with our faith and finding it wanting in terms of its validity, but rather when they have engaged with many of our people, they have found us sorrowfully shallow in our actual understanding of faith.

I find many believers who struggle to give anything but a few inherited and well worn clichés when asked to give a reason for their belief (1 Peter 3:15). This is one of the reasons why so many Salvationists find their faith ship-wrecked when attending university. They find themselves in an alien and even hostile environment, where cliché holds no water and they fall prey to the many challenges the Christian faith is faced with in that world of academia. Those of us in leadership must bear some of this respons-ibility for not investing in the development of our young people's minds: all of us must take responsibility to see the situation change.

What I am not calling for is some arid intellectual stance that fills our minds with mere concepts and 'theories' but rather a vibrant, thinking faith that stands on the rock of God's word and engages credibly with the challenges of the world. For example, a friend of mine once laid out a challenge when preaching that has often come back to haunt me within my Salvationist context. He challenged those present that if they had been a Christian for more than five years, yet could not give a reason when chal-lenged why they believed the word of God to be true and reliable, they were in deep trouble in our increasingly secularised and religiously pluralistic society. Most Salva-tionists I know couldn't provide a credible answer when challenged. They believe in the Bible just because that is what they have always been told. Or take the issue of the historical validity of the resurrection of Christ. Many scholars see this as one of the best attested events in all of antiquity yet most believers that I meet have no idea as to why this is so.

Often I speak in universities and when speaking to 'not-yet-Christian' people, find that they are often very challenged when faced with the vast weight of historical evidence behind the events of the resurrection. The truth is they end up understanding more about the event, than many of those who believe in it and have committed their lives to Christ as a result of it. I don't say this to be overtly critical but rather to raise the important issue for us to be 'thinking warriors'. We must learn to think well, to know why we believe what we believe, so as to be able to stand our ground.

Steps of change

In this part of the battle for the mind, Guinness suggests a number of helpful steps that address this thinking-famine head on.

Repentance – This is the first essential step. We must both individually and corporately repent for not loving God in the way that he calls us to. He has given us incredible minds. Most humans use only an small percentage of their brain's capacity (at times the Church has cut back even on that). Guinness asserts:

> 'We need to confess that we have given ourselves up to countless forms of unutterable folly. God has given us minds but many of us have left them underdeveloped or undeveloped.' [32]

Like any form of sin this needs to be turned away from and choices made that will change how we love God with our minds. I fear that in the Army we have fallen into the trap of anti-intellectualism – denying a thinking faith, identifying genuine searches for truth or understanding as worldly or sinful. Whilst at theological college I met a well-known counsellor and specialist in child development and counselling for abused children who worked with UNICEF and major charities. We talked together, and during the conversation it became apparent that he grew up in the Army and was once even a candidate for officership. When I enquired as to why he did not continue on in this particular journey of vocation, he replied that he had left frustrated, for every time he asked genuine questions of faith and doubt he was told not to bother with such nonsense and just believe. This he found intellectually unacceptable and so left to fulfil another vocation.

The tragedy is that this story could be repeated many times. To think, question, and analyse is not sinful nor lacking in faith but is rather obedience to the law of God to love with the mind. I fear that at times laziness and ignorance have been cloaked under the so-called banner of 'pure faith'. When Jesus told us to have the faith of a child he was not calling us to be childish. Is there anything more enquiring than an inquisitive six-year-old asking the 'why' question? No, childlike trust and relationship is the basis of a faith that is secure enough to ask the tough questions essential to a robust faith in our contemporary world.

We must repent of our lack of wrestling with God's word, the realities of a complex world and how to mesh the two together. We must repent for not loving God in the way he commands and deserves. This must be done by individuals who have left the mind which God has given us under-developed. As with our recent discoveries about the universe via the Hubble telescope that has shown us vast new areas of space previously undreamt of, so we should increasingly engage our minds in the pursuit of God as we encounter undiscovered revelations, that can call us on deeper into relationship and understanding.

I feel our institutions may also have to repent for (in places) not creating a culture of thinking that has left many of our people ill-equipped to face the challenges of a questioning world.

Love – The second step. We need to discover then in reality what it means to love God with our mind, and what it means to think Christianly. Guinness again helps us in this regard:

> 'Thinking Christianly is thinking by Christians about anything and everything in a consistently Christian way – in a manner that is shaped, directed and restrained by the truth of God's Word and God's Spirit.' [33]

By this I do not mean by following a particular denominational line on specific issues, nor a mere repetition of so-called orthodoxy. Rather it is an engagement with issues that fully utilises and stretches the minds we have been given. Put simply the question that must guide all our thinking, and focus our love for him with our minds is 'What does Jesus think?'

The mind is a mix of intellectual light and spiritual ardour, and must lead us to develop what Dorothy Sayers has called a mind 'in love.' Those of us who at any stage have been infatuated with another human being will realise that at the point of its greatest intensity, all issues of life are drained through the sieve of our relational obsession. So too, as we love God our thinking is increasingly shaped and moulded by the intensity of that love. The difference being that as we become infatuated it often blinds us to reality, but as we love God more, so our engagement and understanding of reality increases. Jesus states in John 8:31–32:

> *'If you hold to my teaching, you are really my disciples. Then you will know the truth, and the truth will set you free.'*

This says two important things. Firstly, obedience to his revealed will is the doorway to good thinking. Secondly, the word translated 'truth' could faithfully be translated 'reality'. Once you engage with reality through obedience, this will set you free to be fully who you were created to be. This is something of what it means to love God with our minds.

Wisdom and foolishness – The obedient warriors find themselves living in the paradox of apparent sense and senselessness. At times our spirit-guided choices will appear foolish to the wisdom of the world in which we live. The values of the Kingdom of God are often at such a counter-point to the predominant culture, that we appear credulous to those looking on and must face the cost of what it will mean to look a fool for the sake of Christ (1 Corinthians 1:18, 25).

This said, we must again resist this being a cop-out from working hard with our thinking. All truth is God's truth, all good sense is God's sense. When teaching on sexuality I often begin by pointing out why virginity, celibacy and marital faithfulness are the most 'sensible' choices for a human being wanting to live life to the full. I then go to Scripture to demonstrate that the reason why God calls us to such things, is because we all agree it makes most sense. In the words of the apostle Paul we must *'Be very careful, then, how you live – not as unwise but as wise'* (Ephesians 5:15). Part of the battle for the mind is to have the courage to look foolish in the expression of true wisdom.

Beware the Trojan horse – Laziness is something I struggle with. This becomes positively dangerous when it affects the exercising of my mind. I think for many of us there comes a stage in our Christian life when we can switch to a kind of Christian auto-pilot. We know the rules, written and unwritten. We know what to say, how to act, how to respond, worship and reply when asked about our faith. This form of 'professional Salvationism' has to be one of the most destructive aspects of our corporate culture. It must be continually guarded against. We must make active decisions to be continually moving on in our faith and thinking; adding to the investment of our bank of Christian thinking.

To think like Jesus is a lifetime journey in taking *'captive every thought to make it obedient to Christ'* (2 Corinthians 10:5). Guinness quotes the helpful perspective of Oswald Chambers on this issue of constant battling for the mastery of our minds:

> 'God will not make me think like Jesus, I have to do it myself; I have to bring every thought into captivity to the obedience of Christ.'[34]

If we are honest with ourselves, we are more worldly than we realise in our thinking and assumptions. The battle for the mind is a constant one that needs persistent, active engagement. In the words of Guinness:

> 'Every alien assumption, old or new, is like a Trojan horse in the city of a believer's mind.'[35]

It is said that to 'assume' is to make an 'ass' of 'u and me'! We must ever be watchful for the Trojan horses of our thinking.

The best form of defence is attack

This is not about dismissing or rejecting people, but rather being equipped to face the challenges of a rapidly trans-forming world. The landscape of many of our societies is ever-changing and vigilance is needed to keep a check on our attitudes, lifestyles and presuppositions. We need to proactively see the issues that our faith is going to be facing, and thinking through the consequences of cultural change. In the increasingly pluralistic culture of the West we need incisive thinkers to assist us to map our distinct-iveness beyond shouting louder and reaffirming the rhetoric of previous eras. I remember speaking during a beach mission to someone on the beach mission whom I had assumed was a believer. We talked much about our 'Christ' and it was only as he began to talk about his forms of meditation and spiritual 'channelling' that I realised I was talking to a deeply committed mystic and New Ager. The edges of faith and belief are increasingly blurred and we need to constantly exercise our minds so as to understand. Like the apostle Paul in Athens we must spend time looking carefully (Acts 17:23) at beliefs in our age, so as to be clear about our own faith and also to help others travel towards Christ on their own journey of faith.

To achieve this we will need to develop our personal and corporate curriculum. We will need to study not just God's word, but also other faiths and belief systems. James Sire's book *The Universe Next Door* (published by IVP), is an excellent resource as a starting point in this area. Christian commentaries and contemporary publications on social trends and development, are essential reading for the warriors who want their faith to be ever relevant, and count for something in an increasingly complex world.

We need the real 'thinkers' amongst us (of whom sadly I am not one), to be some of the best thinkers around, providing social comment and analysis to shape the future of our society's policies and culture. We should strive to be viewed like William Wilberforce and his believing contemporaries who were described as a group whose 'brains and brilliancy would not be denied even by those who sneered at their religion.'[36] They were warriors who truly loved God with their minds and were known for doing so.

Starve It!

The mind is like a sponge and soaks up anything within its vicinity. Consequently it needs to be protected from unhelpful influences. This is particularly important in an increasingly visual world that bombards our mind with destructive images. When we read a book or hear a song it may not remain with us for long. Alternatively, when we see an image on paper or particularly on a video screen, that image may stay with us the rest of our lives. The abuse of the TV screen to propagate violence, greed or pornography has seared the consciences of millions who find themselves still living with long-passed watched images. It is a permanent scarring of our emotional make-up and if it has been especially intense, can cause and sustain very destructive habits.

A key strategy for dealing with this and winning the battle for the mind is to starve it of the kind of destructive stimulation that has been influencing its behaviour. This is something I had to come to terms with in my early Christian life. I used to enjoy very violent films, but by the end of them was hyped up to my eyeballs on adrenaline. Not a helpful frame of mind for a riot-squad policeman. One day, having just watched a typical film of this type, my friend pointed this out to me. When I responded in kind, I realised the very negative effect these films were having upon my life. So I covenanted before God that I would not watch them again and, bar one or two lapses, have kept to this.

Job recognised his sexual weakness and in his desire to honour God stated:

> *'I made a covenant with my eyes not to look lustfully at a girl.'* (Job 31:1)

He knew he had to starve an area of weakness to gain victory over it. I have been greatly challenged recently regarding my eating habits. At times I have been gluttonous and put on weight unnecessarily. I have overeaten and at times I think been addicted to over-indulgence. Again there is only one way to beat this issue of the mind; starve it, or fast till you develop new habits and patterns of consumption.

The new absolute for Western society is choice. This is more than just having numerous options to choose from but rather choosing to keep all your options open. This though is not an option for an active warrior. Choosing to withhold certain things from your lifestyle is sometimes an important step in starving those unhelpful habits. Some friends of mine have been part of church networks where new Christians were instructed to burn all their non-Christian records and books. Personally I find this somewhat extreme, yet I want to hold on to the important principle that it lifts up. If your life is controlled by certain habits or addictions then such drastic action may be totally appropriate. I have prayed with numerous young men who were literally addicted to fantasy role-play games. This had become an obsession which consumed their lives. Having prayed with them I recommended that they burn all the materials involved in the game. When they did this, they said that it was an important part of the freeing process.

One of the greatest addictions found in the Church is the addiction to comfort. It has been called the idolatry (worship) of comfort. Making a choice to withhold certain comforts from yourself or even inducing certain hardships to challenge your comfort orientation, is incredibly healthy in assisting the battle for your mind. The ancient Celtic missionaries would sometimes stand in the icy North Sea to meditate, rid themselves of fleshiness, and discipline their minds. I would personally find this unacceptable (the Mediterranean may be more appropriate), yet I want to learn from the only people who successfully evangelised a pagan Britain and saved the islands from barbarism. They were extremists, but highly effective in developing a disciplined spirituality that changed their world.

Some may find this all too extreme, but anyone who has worked with addicts of any kind will know that such action is often necessary. The issue for you may not be alcohol or role-play games, but it could be avoiding excessive eating habits, reading certain materials or keeping away from certain types of shops to avoid impulse buying. Whatever the issue, warriors need to be ever-vigilant to avoid becoming slaves to destructive habits or values. This has nothing do to with legalism, for as Scripture states *'it is for freedom that Christ has set us free'* (Galatians 5:11). Rather it is freedom to choose **not** to give into so many of those things that would seek to enslave us.

Cage It!

I have got a big mouth! There is no point pretending it is not so, or getting hurt when someone suggests it. I am one of life's loud people, a characteristic turned into a distinct disadvantage when coupled with a mouth which some-times moves faster than the brain. James, the half-brother of Jesus, recognised the inherent danger of the tongue and wisely gave strong guidelines for ensuring that the right words came out from it (James 3:1–12).

I have lost count of the number of times when, through bitterness, insecurity or a whole host of other reasons, I have heard destructive words released from someone's mouth causing significant damage. I have met numbers of people that carry an amazingly powerful critical spirit, who, at a moment's notice, will seek to criticise, insult or point out the inadequacy of others. These people are always a drain on churches and teams, and sadly many of them are believers. They rarely come up with any innovation or ideas, but will give ten reasons as to why and how another idea cannot happen. These are the dream-killers, the vision-destroyers whom I feel have been one of the most destructive forces in the Church in recent years. Those who struggle with this militant negativity will have to be honest enough to recognise it within themselves – realism is not always sufficient cover for cynicism. Whether the cause of this character trait is hurt, disappointment, or rampant cynicism it must be healed, confessed or controlled.

This is not just about our words but other behavioural patterns. I know of someone who as a result of their own insecurity, could not walk into a room without seeking to be the centre of attention. This not only consistently annoyed people but limited the growth and development of others. Others in leadership roles may sometimes use the power of their position to exert inappropriate influence over others. This characteristic has a lot to do with their insecurities, ego and pride, and is particularly dangerous when they are trusted people in positions of authority.

When considering this part of our battle we will need to be painfully honest with ourselves. We need to ask who we are, and what aspect of us affects others negatively. One of my own great personal challenges (read weakness), is my sometimes aggressive attitude and character. Much of the time it is not something of which I am consciously aware nor how I intend to be, but too often my intensity level overrides my grace output, and damages others. I have struggled with this for some time as it makes me inaccessible to some of the people I am called to serve. It is not just my words but my body language, voice inflection and general demeanour. I am told by those close to me that this aspect of my character often threatens and disturbs others.

If I am to be an effective warrior this has to change. I have to learn to 'cage in' those aspects of myself that negatively impact others. Our individualistic society rejects such thinking. It proclaims that you should be free to be who you are, and that people should accept you that way. Rubbish! A follower of Jesus has his gracious model as a goal and his life of love and grace is the plumbline. To win my battle part of me may need controlling until it changes.

Wipe It!

To use another computer analogy, when a disc has been corrupted, it needs cleaning off before it is available again for use. This process is known as wiping – the deleting of null and void material that is no longer useful. A similar process is required for many warriors who have 'files' in their computer banks that need to be wiped clean due to their useless or destructive nature. Without such a process a warrior will often be hampered in his warfare role. We must help each other to identify those things within ourselves that if let out could be so destructive. Cage them when in the field of battle, and seek the healing of the Holy Spirit.

One of the most common problems relates to the issue of

guilt. Even though a Christian is part of the company for whom *'there is now no condemnation...'* (Romans 8:1), many carry unnecessary guilt, largely through a lack of understanding of the adequacy of Christ's sacrifice. Often we come to God with current or long-past, but often repented sin, begging that in his mercy he might forgive us. Deep down inside we fear there may come a point when we go just too far and God will give up on us.

Though a common fear it is thankfully so far from the truth: when a child comes to his heavenly Father in genuine repentance, he lavishes his forgiveness upon us. Not, primarily, because of his **mercy**, but because of his character of **justice**. The apostle John reminds us:

> *'If we confess our sins, he is faithful and just and will forgive us our sins and purify us from all unrighteousness.'*
> (1 John 1:9)

Our forgiveness is not based upon any precarious mercy of a benevolent God, but rather a God who is committed in a covenant of justice to forgive us. We are forgiven not on the basis of our pleading, nor just the love of God, but rather since Christ has already paid the debt owed for our sin, God is morally bound to forgive because the price has been paid (1 Corinthians 6:20).

In retailing terms, I walk into a shop, hoping to leave the premises with the product called 'Forgiveness', knowing I have nothing with which to buy it. I am then overwhelmed when I am given the product free by the owner; not because he likes me or is even feeling particularly generous on this day, but simply because his son came in earlier, purchased the product on my behalf and left instructions for it to be handed over to me whenever I came in. Forgiveness is mine by right because the 'just price' has already been paid.

Guilt is totally appropriate for those who have made a decision of the will to rebel against the will of God, and who continue to walk that way in unrepentance. Guilt is entirely inappropriate and irrelevant for the earnest believer who repents, confesses and moves on.

Heaven's eyes

We mentioned earlier the importance of understanding world-views. Accepting that we have been heavily influenced in the 'interior design' of our minds is important, particularly in terms of how that affects our theology and view of spirituality. Tragically we have been deceived in many areas about the true nature of the war, and this I think has had a terrible impact upon our personal and corporate effectiveness in battle. Many of us have viewed reality through the secular eyes of our society, rather than the biblically inspired ones of heaven.

Since the historical period within Europe known as the Enlightenment, the acceptance of a spiritual dimension to reality has been under attack. In the West we have been taught that ultimate reality is only that which can be scientifically seen and touched. In modern thought the spiritual realm and spiritual beings are not real, but belong to the somewhat primitive world of less developed peoples. Although atheists are quite rare in the ranks of the Army, there are many who hold something of the above view. The spiritual realm so clear in Scripture, Church and Army history is seen as inappropriate for so-called modern man, and needs to be laid aside in favour of the understanding of our scientific age.

The worship of science, the uncritical acceptance of this very secular world-view and the impact of rationalistic liberal theology has significantly impacted the Army and the minds of many of its members. However, the truth is that this materialistic view is a minority view within the world. Most people work with an understanding of a physical and spiritual reality that interface in many areas of life, which is the true Salvationist theology and world view. Where we have owned this humanistic perspective that has stripped the spiritual dynamic from our thinking, it must be wiped clean.

The apostle Paul speaks to the Ephesian Christians very clearly about the true nature of the spiritual battle:

> *'Finally, be strong in the Lord and in his mighty power. Put on the full armour of God so that you can take your stand against the devil's schemes. For our struggle is not against flesh and blood, but against the rulers, against the authorities, against the powers of this dark world and against the spiritual forces of evil in the heavenly realms.'*
>
> (Ephesians 6:10–12)

He was talking to the church led by Timothy in Ephesus which was facing direct confrontation with the powers of spiritual evil and darkness. This city, a centre of cultic worship and pagan culture, was rife with destructive spiritual influences, so Paul was educating them how best to engage in this spiritual war.

Major Chick Yuill has dealt with this subject at length in his excellent book *This Means War!* therefore I will not major on it here, but simply mention it, as such an important part of the battle is for the mind. I have met many Salvationists who do not even believe in the existence of a personal devil nor a spiritual reality with which we need to engage. This I find incredible. We have no rationale for existence outside of a commitment to wage war against these evil spiritual forces. These people, sincere as they are, are in the wrong organisation. There is no room in an Army which is engaged in battle, for people who don't believe the war even exists.

Yes, we must avoid extreme perspectives that see demons in tea cups and give the devil credit for things that are not his. I have heard the phrase 'Oh the devil made me do it' often, to describe what in reality are merely self-centred actions and attitudes. Yet I fear our danger is at the exact opposite end of the scale; we have been duped into **not** believing such beings are a reality. Is there anything more dangerous than an enemy that you don't believe even exists? An enemy that is the source of all the unimaginable evil within the world and who is the adversary of our souls. The same being who led worship in heaven, tempted Adam and Eve, tempted Jesus in the desert, and manifested in the life of Legion, is the same being that rages against the work of the Kingdom of God and the life of every earnest warrior today.

Increasingly I encounter direct opposition in the lives of individuals. Whether it be people who are actually demonised and oppressed by evil spirits, or corps that have been torn apart through division and hate, the war is as real in the Army today as it has ever been. Regularly we are asked to pray with individuals who have been infected by evil spirits and have been affected by evil forces in one way or another. Without engaging in this spiritual warfare against the blindness upon the eyes of unbelievers (2 Corinthians 4:4) they cannot get saved. Without praying against the oppressive and evil influences at work within individuals' lives they will remain in bondage to them. I believe a battle rages for the future of this Movement, and without praying for the spiritual heart of it we will wither and die.

Our real battle is a spiritual one. The evil forces behind oppressive governments, child abuse, spiritual confusion, denominational decline etc., must be challenged in the spiritual realm. We have been given spiritual weapons to fight in this battle (2 Corinthians 10:4) and only they can prevail in this war. Too often I have found myself tackling spiritual dynamics in an inadequate way. To tackle spiritual forces with merely 'carnal' weapons is the equivalent of coming out against the hi-tech Army that fought in the Gulf War, with a pea-shooter. Our minds must be attuned to the spiritual reality of the war. All the church growth principles, planned giving programmes, and evangelistic campaigns in the world, will be of no use unless they are carried on the wings of prayer.

The early Army regularly wrestled late into the night for individuals and situations. They knew where the real war lay. Prayer doesn't **make** a difference, prayer **is** the difference. The phenomenal growth of the charismatic and

Pentecostal church who have embraced this theology speaks of its importance. In 1945 it counted 16 million adherents world-wide, by 1965 it had grown to 50 million and by 1991 had grown to an incredible figure of 391 million. Just one Pentecostal denomination, the Assemblies of God, has registered the incredible growth of 1.6 million to 13.2 million between 1965 and 1985. They have embraced the spiritual warfare theology of the early Army, and some of our early evangelists like Gypsy Smith and Smith Wigglesworth became some of their most influential historical figures.

Primarily this is an issue of the mind. Wiping unbiblical perspectives and embracing biblical truth, is an important step in the battle for the mind. A militant spiritual warfare theology that is strongly grounded in Scripture, is the only hope for the future of this movement. It is essential to our evangelistic and transformational effectiveness; it is the only thing that makes sense of our military metaphor. To hold another view is to betray our roots and leave the oppressed and unsaved in darkness.

Reverse It!

When Jesus launched his ministry manifesto in what has come to be known as the Sermon on the Mount, he described a whole new way of being (Matthew 5–7). His words were at counterpoint to the predominant culture of the day, ethically, morally and relationally. This statement of intent has provided the platform for distinctive Christian living for 2000 years, and its power is still as dynamic and stark as ever. Warrior living is by definition 'counter cultural'. Part of our reason for being, is to provide a vision for a new 'way of being', a visual metaphor of what could and should be.

At its heart is the distinction between 'adherence' and 'conversion'. There are many in our world who adhere to all sorts of belief systems. They need have no real impact on how they live in the home or work-place day by day, but is rather a compartmentalised 'spiritual' bit of their life. In philosophical terms this would be known as a form of 'dualism'; separating the physical/social aspects of our lives from the religious. Tragically this is all too common within Salvationist circles. The fact that people are part of this movement seems to have little affect on how they live and work within their career or neighbourhood. This is not being judgmental, but just stating an obvious part of the culture of a rapidly declining denomination in the Western world.

Conversion alternatively involves repentance and a complete about-turn into a new way of being. This affects every aspect of lifestyle and belief, and begins a process of sanctification and transformation that 'reverses' many of the habits and values of a pre-conversion existence.

I believe that the most powerful way to win the battle for the mind is to go on the offensive. This means applying the counter-cultural principles of Jesus, and choosing to live in the opposite spirit to that with which you are struggling. If it is greed, give away; gluttony, fast; selfishness, serve; laziness, hard discipline etc. The way to seeing our minds renewed, is to put in place in our lives new values and ideals, and then being in a community of people who will help us live them out.

Hit Where It Hurts

Possibly one of the greatest challenges facing warriors in the Western world, is how we view the heinous injustice of wealth and resource distribution within the world; in particular our own level of consumption, and for many the unquestioned trend of financial upward mobility. This has something to do with how we give, and it has everything to do with how we think.

Jim Wallis talks about his 'Conversion to the Poor', as a second conversion experience. His evangelical upbringing had well grounded him in the Bible, but little had been done to address the cultural lenses through which he viewed reality. He came to realise that in a world rampant with injustice, when put alongside God's revelation in this world we, like God himself, had to choose to side with the poor. The question is, whose side are we on? How do we 'think' on this issue? It is an issue of the mind and is a fundamental issue of identity and obedience for any committed warrior, particularly within a movement like The Salvation Army.

Pilgrimage

Wallis asserts that we 'get converted' when we pilgrim to places where we don't normally belong. This was certainly the case for me. One of the most powerful experiences of my life and certainly one of the most foundational to my thinking, was a visit to the country of Ethiopia in the mid-1980s. Nothing had prepared my mind for what I was to encounter there. The experiences of poverty, death and desolation were beyond anything I had previously encountered. Hopelessness was inescapable. Life had stripped people of dignity to the extent that it was normal for young children to be crippled at birth by their parents in order to make them better beggars.

Amidst the overwhelming stench of degradation, one moment haunts me still. Walking across a road, I looked out of the corner of my eye and saw what I thought was a pile of brown rags. Nothing seemed out of the ordinary until I saw this pile move. On closer inspection I realised it was a young woman sitting begging with her child in her arms. I initially thought the child was dead, but as I approached, it moved slightly. Even though we had been warned by local missionaries not to give out money to beggars, I was not able to walk past without responding in some way. I squatted down in front of her. She lifted her head and I looked into her eyes. I think for the only time in my life I looked into an empty void. She had eyes, but there was nothing there. No emotion, no dignity, no humanness. I must have squatted there for about thirty seconds looking into this woman's face. She dropped her head and hid the money in her rags. I turned and walked away.

That experience has stayed with me. When I returned to this country I found it difficult walking into food stores, abundant with choice. I struggled to work out what was happening within me. Every time I looked at a friend's child who was about the same age as the one the woman had been carrying, I would cry. I spent an hour and a half weeping on a friend's front room floor. The questions I began to ask were uncomfortable. Looking back I realise why: I had no answers. What I had known of the Christian life up until that point, had nothing to say of relevance for that young woman. I returned from Africa at 10 pm on Friday; at 10 am on Saturday I was in London, on the March for Jesus, surrounded by thousands of other Christians just like me. One question tormented my mind: 'How does what I am doing now connect with what I have just come from?'

People kept telling me:

'There is nothing you can do.'

'The problem is just too big.'

'Poverty is all just relative.'

I didn't believe that then. Many years later, having studied the word of God and world affairs in much greater depth, I definitely don't now. The one thing the Church cannot do is '**nothing**.'

The net result of my experiences in Ethiopia has been an incredible transformation in my thinking and lifestyle. The way in which I view my family, my possessions and my job has been radically altered. Whether or not they are still alive, for my Christian faith to make sense it must be conducted with reference to that woman and her child and the millions like them. This is part of my conversion, not as some shallow gospel of works, but rather a part of the conversion process of being turned more into the likeness of Jesus.

I am sure much of the above could be dismissed as the guilt-ridden ramblings of an over-stressed evangelist trying to live with his own compromise. Yet for those wishing to seek comfort for themselves by such a dismissal, this dismissal is not even a mild possibility. An essential issue in the battle for the mind of any warrior wishing to make a difference to the next millennium, **has** to be the role that the poor play in our lives. In a society which drives us towards individual gain and personal ambition, both the Church and the individuals who make up that Church, must live in an opposite manner. It is only in this way that we will most effectively challenge those around us.

Scripture makes it clear that the poor, and the issues of injustice relating to the poor, **have** to be a major concern of every warrior. Throughout the Bible, the people of God are judged for two primary reasons: idolatry and the oppression of the poor – often as a result of idolatry. This aspect of God's revelation must be the plumbline by which our faith and ministry is understood and worked out. I have heard it suggested that concern for social justice was primarily an Old Testament issue and that God in his progressive revelation had moved onto to more important 'spiritual matters' in the New Testament. This is heretical nonsense. God has a bias towards the poor, not because he doesn't like the middle-class, but because no-one else is on their side. Jesus made his feelings clear, aligning the treatment of the poor and marginalised with our treatment of himself.

> *'When the Son of Man comes ... he will separate the people one from another as a shepherd separates the sheep from the goats. He will put the sheep on his right and the goats on his left. Then the King will say to those on his right, "Come, you who are blessed by my Father; take your inheritance ... For I was hungry and you gave me something to eat, I was thirsty and you gave me something to drink, I was a stranger and you invited me in, I needed clothes and you clothed me, I was sick and you looked after me, I was in prison and you came to visit me." Then the righteous will answer him, "Lord when did we see you hungry and feed you, or thirsty and give you something to drink? When did we see you a stranger and invite you in, or needing clothes and clothe you? When did we see you sick*

> *or in prison and go to visit you?" The King will reply, "I tell*
> *you the truth, whatever you did for one of the least of these*
> *brothers of mine, you did for me ... "'*
>
> (Matthew 25:31–40)

No matter how hard we try to rationalise or contextualise this passage into insignificance, it is inescapable. In short Jesus says, 'What you do or don't do for them is what you do or don't do for me.' Plain and simple to understand – much more difficult to live out. Yet if we are to be faithful to our call, we must try. Mother Theresa spoke so powerfully of this principle, declaring that whenever she picks a drunk or drug addict out of the gutter and looks into their eyes, she doesn't see the drink or drugs looking back at her but the very eyes of Jesus himself. In Washington, USA, there is a welfare worker who serves on a bread line for the homeless. She prays the same prayer each day as they serve the poor: 'Lord we know you are going to be walking in this line today. Help us to treat you well.' That woman, Mother Theresa and many others have understood that when all the rhetoric of battle, theology of cultural engagement and passionate worship is over, the acid test of a warrior lifestyle is how we treat the poor and marginalised.

In *The General Next to God*, William Booth's early encounter with poverty is recalled, which developed within him a holy 'revulsion of poverty.' He was not only called to reach and serve the poor but was driven to it by a burning heart of passion that had gripped his mind and will.

Richard Collier records the story of how Bramwell called at the house and found his father's braces flying like the wings of Pegasus:

> ' "Did you know that men slept out all night on the
> bridges?" ... The Salvation Army couldn't tackle every
> social evil ... but Booth with one angry sweep ...
> silenced his arguments. His command was a finality
> destined to alter The Salvation Army's entire future:
> "Go and do something! We must do something ... Get

hold of a warehouse and warm it and find something to cover them." '[37]

This is our inheritance as a movement as well as our biblical mandate. We only exist because many Victorian churches had done much to exclude the poor. Honest questions have to be asked as to how true to this call we have been. Whilst we are the biggest voluntary provider of social care in both the UK and the USA, the extent to which the average Salvationist has a concern and involvement with the poor is questionable. Most people seem to have a starry-eyed view of the average Salvationist being out on the streets 24 hours a day feeding the homeless, somehow fitting in another job on top of this. The truth is the vast majority of Salvation Army officers and soldiers have absolutely nothing to do with the poor and marginalised. There are obvious exceptions to this rule within Social Services and some corps settings, but for most of us it is the norm. They just play no part in our lives.

I know some people who have a very obvious gifting and calling to care for the marginalised. Whilst they are hugging and comforting I am just standing there with a kind of embarrassed sense of impotency. I could easily allow this to become my cop-out, my very spiritualised excuse for lack of concern and selfishness. Yet Scripture will not allow me to do so. I am Salvation Army, I am a follower of Jesus and consequently I need to be deeply committed in my mind and subsequent actions to the things that are high on his priority list.

Can we be sure that a modern-day version of the prophet Amos's thunderous challenge cannot be addressed to ourselves?

> I hate, I despise your praise and worship celebrations,
> I cannot stand your incestuous conferences.
> Even though you bring me Christmas collections and
>   harvest offerings,
> I will not accept them.

Though you bring me choice books and videos
I will have no regard for them.
Away with the noise of your songsters and choirs
I will not listen to the music of your worship or brass
  bands.
But let justice roll on like a river, righteousness like a
  never-failing stream.

(Amos 5:21–24 paraphrased)

His challenge was to a group of religious people whose priorities and lifestyle were a long way short from the rhetoric of their religious pronouncements and public face. The challenge, although a difficult one, must be faced.

The mind to give

For those of us in the West comfort is the expected norm, so to change this destructive trend is going to require decisions in the mind that hurt and dramatically transform the way we live. I shall mention giving in a later section, but I talk here in terms of the management of our budgets and the destinations of our resources. I recently presented the Bible studies at the leadership day of the World Vision (UK) development charity. Something I mentioned on that day has come back to haunt me ever since. I asked them whether or not the staff of that organisation could comfortably send a copy of their own personal bank statements with the latest fund-raising appeal letter. This is an important issue of personal integrity. For those of us in The Salvation Army we must ensure we 'outgive' those we ask to contribute to the work we do.

Intelligent giving is essential and to assist in the process it should be targeted and informed. Regular giving to a known programme, nation or project helps motivate us in our levels of sacrificial stewardship. We can see the difference our giving is making which may even motivate us to recruit others to the cause. If it is possible, visit the destination of your support. We should own it not only in terms of a banking order, but emotionally and prayerfully.

The mind to serve

A question to be asked by every person with skills needed within the poorer areas of our own nations or further afield is: 'Should I go there?' The priority given to our career must be dethroned for a perspective that sees those skills available for God to use wherever he requires. Doctors, nurses, teachers, engineers, accountants and increasingly computer experts are all desperately needed in many places. We need to honestly ask the question: 'Are we building a life or a lifestyle?' There is a huge difference. So often those of us with education and opportunity follow the expected path of our upwardly-mobile culture.

As I have been writing this section I have been on the telephone to a friend of mine who is a well qualified teacher. He is considering the possibility of giving up his comfortable job in London and going to Liberia – at present one of the most dangerous and unstable nations in the world – to teach children who have no teachers. I quote part of our conversation:

> 'Well, here I am in my nice comfortable Western middle-class lifestyle while those kids have absolutely nothing. I have the skills they need and could really make a difference in that place. Yes, it's risky but so what? Someone has to do the job.'

I asked him all the cautious questions that someone in my position is supposed to ask in those types of conversations but inwardly I was leaping around with excitement. Here we have a Christian with every opportunity to build a comfortable and successful teaching career in the UK, yet he senses the tug of the Spirit upon his heart. This is not to decry those who are called to stay, but rather to challenge all who have or are acquiring such skills to ask these types of questions. If I'm not called to **stay** maybe I should **go**.

The mind to cry out

There cannot be many people who have watched a TV or

film production portraying horrendous injustice who have not cried out verbally or emotionally against the injustice they have just witnessed. I remember watching the film *Cry Freedom* about the life of the South African activist Steve Biko, and the abuse he suffered at the hands of racist and bigoted authorities. I recall seething inside as I sat and observed the list of black South Africans who had died in police custody, as their names were reeled off at the end of the film. My whole being was enraged with a sense of injustice and cried out for things to be different. Although many will relate to my experience, sadly too few of us have translated those responses into action as part of our Christian life and witness.

One of the proudest moments of our Salvation Army history was when William Stead and Bramwell Booth were involved in uncovering the horrendous evil of child prostitution, and brought about major legislative change to protect abused children. This act of advocacy and cry for justice transformed the lives of many of those children, and protected thousands who would have been at risk. This role of speaking out is an integral part of what it means to be a warrior in the Kingdom.

Tragically the Church has often neglected this aspect of its prophetic calling, and somehow has developed a twisted theology that sees socio-political involvement as somehow worldly and not the work of the people of God. Yet nothing could be further from the truth in terms of our biblical and denominational heritage. As Martin Luther King stated so powerfully and uncomfortably at the height of the civil rights struggle in America:

> 'This generation will not be judged for the evil the bad people have done, but rather for the appalling silence of the good.'

He understood, as every prophet has, that God's primary voice is his Church, the army of God.

> *'Is not this the kind of fasting I have chosen: to loose the*
> *chains of injustice and untie the cords of the yoke, to set*
> *the oppressed free and break every yoke? Is it not to share*
> *your food with the hungry and to provide the poor wanderer*
> *with shelter – when you see the naked, to clothe him, ... If*
> *you do away with the yoke of oppression, with the pointing*
> *finger and malicious talk, and if you spend yourselves on*
> *behalf of the hungry and satisfy the needs of the oppressed,*
> *then your light will rise in the darkness ... '*
>
> (Isaiah 58:6–7, 9–10)

Taking this application one step further, we need to understand the central place fasting played in the Jewish religious scene. It was considered most 'correct,' undoubtedly pious and a clear sign of the spirituality of those participating. This worship that had so much of the 'form' of acceptability appears to be unacceptable to God. The prophet makes it clear that no matter how great our music, how shiny our shoes, how energetic our worship or how 'sound' we might be in our theological thinking – outside of a life that identifies or concerns itself with, serves and speaks for the poor, it is all an empty sham.

Getting Involved

It makes no sense for an organisation like our own to spend all our valuable energies and resources dealing with the symptoms and fruits of injustice whilst ignoring the causes behind it. As the Roman Catholic Bishop Romero stated:

> 'When I feed the poor they call me a saint, when I ask why the poor are hungry they call me a Communist.'

He understands, like we need to, that our role is not merely to fight against the manifestations of poverty but also to challenge the unjust systems, structures and people that cause it in the first place.

The term 'apolitical' has traditionally provided the

framework for Salvationist thinking within the socio-
political arena. It means that our politics should not be
defined by worldly party-political agendas, but rather God's
call for us to be instruments of change in bringing about
justice and his *'shalom'* (peace, wholeness) to the world.
This inevitably means that we must not, cannot, dare not
avoid involvement in the arena of politics, economics and
social concern. For some this will mean a life of involvement in terms of their vocation and sense of call. For
others it will mean using our voting and spending power to
influence for good, at times taking part in large initiatives,
in terms of advocacy on behalf of others. For many
Christians it has meant direct confrontation with those in
power, no matter what the cost. Just recently a number of
Christian leaders known to me were arrested in America
for their peaceful demonstration regarding the apparent
injustice of the US government, which was cutting taxes
for the rich and powerful, but making benefit cuts for those
most in need within the nation.

We see throughout the book of Acts civil disobedience
was par for the course for the average 'up-and-at-them'
believer, including Paul, who suffered a criminal's death.
The prophetic tradition of the people of God demands such
involvement. I fear that too often an apolitical stance has
meant we have remained silent when we should have been
screaming from the rooftops for justice.

When writing this chapter I had just read about the
confession of The Salvation Army's admission of guilt to
South Africa's Truth and Reconciliation Commission. Our
guilt was not in relation to what we did but rather in not
speaking out, in what we didn't do. This for me was a
proud moment of our history.

I strongly feel that increasingly we need to be involved in
issues of advocacy and social concern. Firstly, because it is
an important role for the people of God which has been left
alone in too many situations. Secondly, the world is
increasingly unjust, so for any Christian warfare to be
effective there will have to be a consideration of how to

engage in this aspect of the war. Thirdly, these aspects of society are increasingly important amongst the younger generation, who loathe injustice and are more animated than many in their response to it. One of the most stark memories of the 1990s in the UK, was the sight of many young teenage girls who were trying to stop the export of live animals for slaughter, being dragged off the road by big burly police officers. I envisage a day when corps and churches will divide not over issues of theology, eschatology or pneumatology but rather the levels of involvement in the socio-political arena. 'What do you mean you are not involved in fighting for the rights of child slaves? Call yourself a Christian?' could perhaps become a common statement made in the Church of the future. People will never care what we know until they know how much we care.

Living parable

On one particular night when it was very cold I was working with the homeless in London. One of the women didn't have any shoes on and in conversation with her I commented that if she didn't rectify the situation her feet could fall off in the cold. She said to me, 'Well it wouldn't matter. In fact it wouldn't really matter if I died.' For a moment I was stuck for what to say and eventually forced out some kind of nice Christian cliché about the fact that she did matter to us and she mattered to God. She just threw her head back in disdain and walked off.

I was deeply disturbed by this event and so when I was back in the centre of town a few days later, I was intent on finding her. I was unable to do so but later that day with some friends who were running a Christmas meal, we prayed that we would find this woman. As we went to leave the venue to invite people in, I opened the door and there was this woman standing on the doorstep. Her comments are not repeatable when I told her we had just been praying for her, but she allowed us to take her home. She spent the night with us and next day went to stay with a family in our corps who care for people in similar situations. She spent Christmas with them and became part of their extended family for a short time. Early in the new year she made a commitment to follow Christ and now is back in her home environment and happily married; a fairy-tale ending. Yet what she said to me shortly after her commitment is still today one of the most challenging statements anyone has ever made to me on this war issue of serving and caring for the poor. She said:

> 'You know when you said to me that I mattered to you and God I thought you were just another Jesus jerk, because we get a lot of those on the streets who just want to come and talk to us about the love of God. But, because I was taken home that night, because I received so much love and care, because I spent Christmas with that young family, I know now that what you say about the love of God is true.'

A lifestyle that does not include the poor in one way or another is not truly engaged with the war. In the words of my friend it must carry the label 'Jesus jerk'.

Principles of Involvement

Mike Morris in his helpful book *Christian Citizenship* outlines three styles of involvement allowing for a diversity of response to the multifaceted nature of many political/ social and economic issues.

The prophets

Like the prophets of old, there are those who feel very deeply about the injustices done to other people. They are passionate in their denunciation of injustice and often find it an all-consuming issue that infects others and even inspires them to action. They need to be those who can move from the articulated critique of a situation into creating appropriate responses and images of lifestyle and action, that in themselves provide a prophetic polemic to the issue being addressed.

The link between proclamation and action is essential to earth the reality of the heartfelt action and empathetic stance. The prophet must stir people to action and engagement with the issue. Part of the contemporary challenge of a global media world is the emergence of 'compassion fatigue'. Many have been stirred by the images that have been thrust in our faces on TV screens, but have felt powerless and resigned to the 'inevitability' of a situation. The prophet must 'call out and call on' to action, if this phenomenon is to be avoided. Prophecy without teeth is merely empty rhetoric.

The politicians

These are not necessarily actual parliamentarians; on the contrary, so much of the most effective lobbying is undertaken by lay people. These may not be the high-profile, up-front types, but rather those who will do all the tedious research in gathering fuel for action. Historically the Church has not always spoken out when it should. Unfortunately at times when it has spoken, it has been ill-informed and has lacked the authority and credibility to cause change.

William Wilberforce was unrelenting in his political struggle against the evil of slavery. He was well informed and understood clearly the real issues at stake, so that when he spoke and lobbied, he did so on a bedrock of knowledge and understanding. In many societies across the world there is a desperate need for a voice to be raised, and political action mobilised within the systems and structures, to give a voice to those who do not have one.

Pastors

These are the people I personally stand in awe of. Those who can just sit, listen, embrace and befriend people in need. Morris describes these as those with 'open hearts and open homes.' People are never too much trouble, time is always available and they don't mind listening to the same story repeatedly. I struggle to concentrate first time round, thinking what I should say next and even at times forgetting people's names. Pastors on the other hand, have an amazing ability to empathise, beyond just an emotional sympathy, and are able to truly connect with people in need.

These people put the warmth of flesh and bones on action, and can begin to pour back into people's lives something of the love deficit they have experienced. Pastors are not normally the best people to tackle the political or prophetic roles, but are an essential aspect of this three-pronged response to socio-political engagement.

Wherever you would place yourself in this mix of prophets, politicians and pastors, the following would be important for all who desire to have their lives count in this way.

- **Be informed** – Ignorance has never been a very effective weapon in warfare.
- **Network** – Connect with organisations that are already involved in the particular issue you are interested in. Whether it be *Amnesty International*, *Christian Solidarity*, *Jubilee Action* or other such groups, don't try and reinvent the wheel. Learn from those who have already learnt from their mistakes. To objections that we shouldn't be involved with non-Christian groups, I answer that I am convinced that God does not care who feeds the poor or who fights for justice, so long as **someone** does.
- **Community** – Whether it be within the context of a local corps or a house group, don't work alone. These are truly spiritual battles we are fighting and it needs more than a few isolated individuals to engage in them. The more people that own a vision the more potent the impact.
- **Be consistent** – For many of us we go through 'fads of compassion'. Justice is not a project, it is at the very heart of the gospel. When I was a police officer I was on duty at an animal rights march. I got talking with

one of the demonstrators and he informed me that they were protesting against all animal products and trades. When I enquired as to why he was wearing leather boots he replied, 'Oh I bought these before I was an animal rights activist!' Make sure your life does not kill your words.

- **Count the cost** – Inevitably when challenging the oppression and wrong actions of one group upon another, there may well be a price to be paid.

Joanna Wilson came into the public eye by breaking into a British Aerospace hanger and damaging a Hawk Fighter Jet. This was in opposition to the sale of the jets to the Indonesian Government who were using them to commit genocide upon their own people in East Timor. Her motivation came from her Christian commitment.

'This concern came from my Christian faith. It was literally through my reading of the Bible that I got involved ... my faith is very much about working for peace and justice.'

She encountered a situation whereby the laws of a country were not just, and they cut across her biblical faith.

'From my faith it is always wrong to kill people, particularly by mass murder and genocide. If I could do something to prevent that, then that would be more important than to remain within the letter of the law.'

Having broken into the factory, she and others disabled the Jet and then sat and waited for the security guards, welcoming them with open arms. When the case went to court an historic decision was reached which acquitted them under law, because they were deemed to have been using reasonable force to prevent a crime (1967 Criminal Law Act).

Although acquitted she knew there could have been a heavy price to pay:

> '. . . even if we had not been acquitted I would never-theless still feel I had done the right thing.'

The cost had been counted. Some Salvationists may pull back at this point insisting upon a 'law-abiding-citizen' approach, yet to do so is to ignore history. Right around the world Salvationists established the rights for freedom of worship and expression in the street through breaking the laws of the land. Our involvement with William Stead over the child prostitution issue involved stepping over legal lines. Although rare, it could be that, as in the past, some of our greatest impacts around the world may come through lifting up the higher law of God and living with the consequences. I am not encouraging people to break the law, but I am saying that our commitment to the laws of God must always be resolute and unquestioning when faced with such challenges. No quarter can be given to allowing our minds to be enslaved by the spirit of the day.

Some may think that much of what has preceded is out of place in a chapter on the battle for the mind. Yet it is in the mind that so much is lost and won, and where the thought processes are that lead to our decisions of lifestyle. The evangelist/sociologist and modern day prophet Tony Campolo affirms the importance of this link between thought and lifestyle.

> 'The greatest cause of atheism today is Christians. Christians who affirm the lordship of Jesus with their minds and lips on Sunday then go out and deny him with their lives on Monday. That is what an unbelieving world finds totally unbelievable.'

The enormity of John Newton's 'mind transformation' had an incredible impact upon his world and those of his contemporaries. What had once been his source of wealth became the driving force of his vision for justice for enslaved peoples.

The fruit of our minds is what manifests in our lives day by day. In many senses we are what we think. Consequently the battle for the mind is one that must be won.

Chapter 3

Battle for the Heart

Loving as a warrior should love

It was the summer of '95. My wife and I were coming to terms with the joys, tears and the sleepless nights of the arrival of our second child. Yasmin was born in June at a healthy 7lb 2ozs, and both her looks and her lungs resembled that of her father. The sounds and smells of having her around had changed our family life dramatically. Her older brother, then three, swayed between overwhelming adoration and robust wrestling; sibling rivalry was developing rapidly. It was a time of warmth, laughter and enjoying the beautiful gift of a child. Yet into the midst of this new family environment came an experience that was to challenge and I believe change me forever in terms of my understanding of the battle for my heart.

One evening, when Yasmin was just eight weeks old, my wife had just given her a Vitamin K liquid capsule drug to help to thicken her blood. The phone rang and Wendy left me with Yasmin to answer it. She was lying on the floor, apparently quite contented and gurgling away as normal. Then, within what appeared to be seconds, she began to choke quite violently. I picked her up, patting her back hoping to ease the irritation, but to no avail. It got worse. She choked and retched and, not knowing what to do, I called Wendy off the phone. The choking eased momentarily but began again with increased intensity. Then within about sixty seconds Yasmin lost consciousness and all her body colour. I phoned for an ambulance and we just sat waiting at the bottom of our stairs praying over our little one. As *her breathing and heart rate slowed to an imperceptible rate we both thought that our little girl was dying before our eyes and there was nothing we could do. The ambulance arrived, the paramedic looked at our daughter and immediately rushed her into the vehicle, secured her in a stretcher and then with the blue lights flashing we were rapidly on our way to the hospital.*

Many things were rushing through my mind as I held my tearful wife's hand. All the scenes from the birth, arrival home, my son holding her, having her fall asleep on my chest, flashed before my eyes. Looking down at Yasmin through my own tear-filled and frightened eyes I was desperately praying for God to keep her alive. As I did so I caught myself praying the following prayer: 'Lord Jesus, even if my Yasmin dies I want you to know that I will not turn away. I will still follow you.' I shook my head, almost questioning my own sanity, and continued to pray for the restoration of our child. We arrived at the hospital and the very efficient medical staff quickly diagnosed Yasmin as merely having a choking fit and then fainting. She stayed in hospital overnight for check-ups, and now as I write is a very robust and energetic two year old. (She still looks like her father.)

I have hesitated to include this story because outside of the context of relationship it could so easily be misunderstood. I have mentioned it purely to illustrate my own battle for the heart and the nature of the issues involved. I have reflected many times on the bizarre and almost absurd prayer that went through my mind in one of the worst moments of my life. Still to this day I do not know why I said what I did and, more importantly, if I would keep to it. I am certain that that would be my intention.

What I do know is that it is at this level of intensity and commitment that the battle for the heart is won and lost. When Jesus said we should love God 'with all our heart' it was an issue of unconditional ownership that was at stake. Uncompromising love for God and commitment to him is the only nesting place for the heart of a warrior. All warriors must regularly examine themselves and ask the question: 'Who owns my heart?'

Duty Calls

This is a challenging question for all believers and in particular Salvationists who talk much about 'doing our duty'. One of the dangers of our military metaphor is the tendency not to work from a position of intimate love but rather a dry sense of duty. The history of military campaigns shows that those fighting from the devotion to their families will often defeat conscripts 'merely doing their duty'; the Russians in Afghanistan would be a case in point. Warriors of God must be driven by a deep, passionate love for God. As the apostle Paul states 'The love of Christ compels us' (2 Corinthians 5:14). Only that will stay the course of the conflict. It was that which drove the early Army in the past and only the same will secure our future.

All every warrior does must come out of a heart of deep love and devotion to Jesus Christ. Loving God may seem a very basic place to start yet it is fundamental to the issues at stake. We are called to love God more than anything else in life; friends, family, work, church and even ourselves. We are called into a passionate love affair with the King of all creation who came and gave his all for our sakes. A Father whose heart of love beat for us in such a way, that he sent his own Son to be butchered and abused by a people who didn't ask for or deserve, but most definitely needed Jesus. This love relationship with Christ is the very cornerstone of who a warrior is and it is that relationship which calls us to devotion, sacrifice and death itself for our lost world.

The Golden Calf (or Cadillac)

In every generation there appears a challenge to the Christian life that affects many believers. Whether it be a political ideal, a cultural prejudice or overt persecution, something raises its head as a major opposition to the gospel. This said, there have been some very consistent challenges to the allegiance of the heart throughout the ages; none more so than the 'love of money.'

If we are to take the analysis of the futurist Tom Sine seriously, the love of money propagated by the empty myth of the Western dream is the root of incalculable injustice within our world. He says, when speaking of the impact of an unchecked materialistic ethos of the West:

> 'The reality of the 1980s and 1990s is that our specta-cular consumer party is over. For the past 200 years those of us in the West have been enjoying this party, and we in the United States have had the very best of it. But the new reality is a future in which over half the people on this planet will never get to come to the Western party.' [38]

Scripture never calls money **itself** evil – only the love and greed for it (1 Timothy 6:10). Yet Jesus clearly identified it as his single greatest rival-god in the battle for the hearts of his warriors.

> *'You cannot serve both God and Money.'*   (Luke 16:13)

This is extraordinary to say the least. He could have chosen the benign Baal or the evil Molech, to whom children were sacrificed. Yet from the host of evil deities of demonic or human invention he chose Money, for he understood its inherent power to divert people from righteous living.

I believe no greater weapon of compromise has been used by the enemy to divert people and resources from being used to fight in our war of salvation. I have seen countless believers get caught up in the whirlpool of consumerism and worship at the many fiscal altars within the world. Used right, money is a wonderful 'tool' for the Kingdom. Allowed to get out of perspective, it is a horren-dous tyrant that demands slavish obedience.

The bottom line

In light of his incredible earnings Charles Wesley once said:

'I pray that when I die I will have not have more than ten pounds in my pocket, lest it burn its way into my heart.'

Extreme perhaps, but less so when we remember the words of Jesus when he said:

'For where your treasure is, there your heart will be also.'
(Matthew 6:21)

So often familiarity breeds contempt, yet if we flip the verse around it takes on frightening clarity: 'For where your heart is there your treasure will be also.' An honest look at our financial priorities and investments will often divulge the ownership of our hearts.

It was Dietrich Bonhoeffer who so helpfully highlighted:

'The light of the body is the eye, the light of the Christian is the heart.'[39]

Ownership of this aspect of who we are determines not only much of our actions but more specifically how we view reality.

The bottom line is this: to what extent does our devotion, trust and love of money exceed our devotion, trust and love of God? As we see in Matthew 19:16–22, with Jesus and the Rich Young Ruler, God gives no quarter to the worship of money. The issue is not the money itself, but rather the grip it has on the heart of this young man. 'Surely,' you cry 'you cannot think that someone like me actually loves or trusts in money and possessions the way you have described. I have money in total perspective and it has no grip upon my heart and life; no problem.' Why not take the following test and just see how free you are?

Find the most expensive thing you own. Find someone who needs it. Give it away. Then, in the bathroom mirror, look yourself in the eye and repeat out loud that materialism has no grip upon your heart.

A number of years ago, in a Salvation Army meeting, I challenged people to do just this. There was something of a stunned response to what was obviously the immature and rather extreme ramblings of the slightly unbalanced visiting preacher. After the meeting, however, I was approached by an older lady from the corps. Somewhat nervous, as her eyes were filled with tears, I wondered what I had said to offend her. Nothing prepared me for what she said: 'Jim and I don't own our house, so this is the most expensive thing that we own. We want you to have it. Sell it and use the money for your ministry.' She put something small in my hand, closed my fist around it and walked tearfully back to her husband. There in the palm of my hand was her platinum 22-diamond eternity ring that Jim had given her years before. It was worth a great deal of money. Stunned by what had occurred, I walked up to them both and explained how moved I was that they had been willing to ask the question and go through this particular exercise. As I went to hand the ring back, she was to stun me again. 'No,' she said. 'You must keep the ring, for Jim and I want to be able to say to God that we are free to serve him in any way he wants and there is nothing that we will not give up for him.' They are free. **Are you?**

In the battle for their hearts these warriors have conquered on one of the greatest battlefields that exists, particularly by those of us from the wealthier nations. This has not been a one-off incident for me as people have given away new leather jackets, stereo systems, jewellery, guitars and even a couple of BMW cars (not to me I might add), when faced with this challenge. So what about you? How would you fare in this particular battle for your heart? I challenge you, the reader, to test your heart and see how you fare. Until you do you will never know. One thing is for sure: until this issue is faced by many of us, we will fail to engage in the bigger battle for the lost in our world.

With the increasing influence of MTV and other media phenomena that bombard us with the lies of a culture driven by the twin engines of materialism and consumerism, we must take some radical steps to not only win this battle, but also guard our hearts from further compromise. What follows are just some very practical steps whereby this might be achieved. These are survival tactics for those living in the fiscal jungle.

Freedom of Simplicity

Jesus stated that it was for freedom that we are set free. The challenge is living out that freedom in a context that continually seeks to enslave us. Remaining free or breaking free from the chains of materialism is one of the greatest challenges we face. Once one of the Army's greatest strengths was an almost reckless trust in God for provision, which allowed them to release resources for the work of mission. This has now become a little-known phenomenon in many places.

This commitment to a form of simplicity is an important weapon in fighting this war. Guilt-ridden appeals for money have worn down many, and nullified that impact to transform and reorientate the lifestyles of those to whom the appeal is made. Simplicity may hold the key to long-term victory in this area. Richard Foster the Quaker writer, has written extensively on this issue and comments strongly upon the power of simplicity to transform lives and communities:

> 'How can we respond [to our world] with any degree of integrity and effectiveness? It is the Discipline of simplicity that gives us the basis for developing a strategy of action that can address this and many other social inequities. Individual, ecclesiastical and corporate action can spring from the fertile soil of simplicity.' [40]

This is nothing new for Salvationists, as simplicity is woven into the very fabric of our Movement. A study of our movement's ceremonies: enrolling soldiers, marriage vows and officership covenant, will show they all make reference to the importance of simplicity. They call for commitment to sacrificial denial for the gospel. No commitment is to be undertaken for personal gain.

This is not just an issue of giving but rather it begins with an inward simplicity that manifests itself in an outward expression. It is a recognition of the call of God upon our lives that focuses upon seeking first the Kingdom of God (Matthew 6:25–34). Nothing must be allowed to divert our attention from this focus. We must always strive to put first things first, living a life of clarity and purpose. Envoy Ian Mayhew comments:

> 'The inward reality of a simple lifestyle involves a life free from anxiety or confusion. For many of us this means a kind of joyful unconcern for our possessions. This is not the exclusive domain of the wealthy or poor, it is deeper than that. It comes from an inner spirit of trust. A deep trust that God will act as our father and lead us through what can often be a minefield.' [41]

It is this power to enable us to be focused and undistracted that makes simplicity such a powerful tool for the warrior at war. Richard Foster quotes Dietrich Bonhoeffer who, before he died at the hands of the Nazis said:

> 'To be simple is to fix one's eye solely on the simple truth of God when all concepts are being confused, distorted and turned upside down.' [42]

In a culture that wars against our spirituality and discipleship, we need as much assistance as possible in mapping a clear path and living effectively. Nothing must be allowed to distract us from our wartime footing.

The heart of simplicity is trust. Trust that God **is** our Father who wants to give to his children (Matthew 7:11), that He **is** Jehovah Jireh, the provider God (Genesis 22:14). Trust that he will be true to his word and trust that he is **able** to provide as he has promised (Ephesians 3:20). It is the trust that called the Israelites in the desert to receive daily from God their provision rather than 'stock pile' just in case (Exodus 16:19). It is the trust that enabled the 1st Century Church to 'sell their possessions and give to any in need' (Acts 2:45; 4:34–35). It is the trust that enables us to see the needs of others, meet them in faith and trust God for our own provision for the future. At the heart of trust is radical obedience. Will we obey and trust?

The values of the Kingdom are always counterpoint to those of the flesh and the world. Obedience to live this kind of life opens up a new life of blessing and freedom. It works into us a new spirit of being. It is a spirit that crucifies greed and covetousness. It is a spirit of compassion and outreach. It is a spirit of sensitivity and trust. Foster comments:

> 'Once this inner disposition has taken over our person-ality, material blessings cannot hurt us, for they will be used for the right purposes. We will recognise material goods to be not for us alone, but for the good of all.' [43]

This makes an important point in reminding us that material blessings within the covenant community of God are almost always for the benefit of the wider community, rather than the individual. The stress was on the good of the nation, the tribe, the clan. When Abraham was blessed, so were hundreds of others. The idea that one could cut off a piece of the consumer pie and go off and enjoy it in isolation was unthinkable. Simplicity not only works for us, but serves the wider community as well. Out of the many blessings it brings and the impact it has, the following are particularly important to our wartime consideration.

Simplicity is:

- **An act of faith** – The common lie in our material world is that it is essential to 'invest' well and set something aside for a rainy day. Whilst many of us in the West 'save for a rainy day', many of our Christian brothers and sisters in the developing world are 'praying for a rainy day'. This is not to deny the validity of wise use and investment for resources, but the consistent message of Scripture is that all dependencies upon anything other than the provision of God is foolhardy at best – and an idolatry at worst (Matthew 6:25–34).

- **An act of self-defence** – Only a crazy warrior climbs over the top of a trench and screams 'Go on, shoot! Do your worst.' Living simply helps guard against compromise (Proverbs 10:2).

- **An act of withdrawal** – We are called to be 'in the world but not of it'. Never an easy path to walk, there come times when we need to make choices to withdraw from enemy territory and regroup. Sometimes our involvement in the 'system' actually mitigates against us fighting effectively, if not scoring own goals and killing our own troops by friendly fire. By remaining passive in a Western economy, we may well end up hurting others on our side in the economically disadvantaged parts of the world.

- **An act of solidarity** – This is an active reversal of the above in living lifestyles that work against oppressive and unjust economic systems. By modelling different options we open up possibilities for others to choose to live counter-culturally on the side of those without the power to affect their own economic destinies. In real terms it is also an act of advocacy, speaking and living on behalf of those who don't have a voice in the market place of world economics.

- **An act of sharing** – This is no passive protest, but actually makes decisions of the will that release more resources for those without. Empowerment is the key to resolving/redressing such financial disparities, and can only be done by those who choose to model and act compassionately in terms of their fiscal resources. It turns purchasing power around by buying goods

produced by organisations with more ethical principles of profit sharing, as well as choosing not to buy
those things that perpetuate the imbalance.

- **An act of provocation** – Simplicity provides a provocation for response. So many people are entrenched in
the materialistic rat race, that those who choose to
model a different lifestyle arouse intense curiosity. One
of the strongest witnesses is a people willing to pay
the price of what it means to live distinct from the
predominant culture. It also states very clearly to
the poor that to be a Christian is to be part of their
answer, not their problem (1 John 3:17).

Ideas for a Creative 'Warrior Simplicity' Lifestyle

This may sound great in theory, but can we live such a life?
What models exist, and where do we look for ideas and
inspiration? Richard Foster's two books *Money, Sex and Power*
(published by Hodder & Stoughton) and *Freedom of Simplicity*
(published by Triangle) are excellent resources. The following are some ideas gleaned from these and other sources.

Ceiling standard

GK Chesterton stated:

> 'There are two ways to get enough: one is to continue
> to accumulate more and more. The other is to desire
> less.' [44]

We need to have an ever-increasing commitment to a
'theology of enough'. That is, we choose to buy what we
need, rather than what we are **told** we need by the adverts
which surround us. Our planet cannot cope with the
continuous over-consumption of the West and consequently is desperately in need of a group of people who
will live and model something different.

Budgeting is a key to effective simplicity and the setting of a standard of living. The clear pattern of most prosperous societies is 'the more you have, the more you spend.' However, rather than hungering to have, we could 'live to give.' I know of a Christian businessman who, when beginning his own business, covenanted with his wife before God to adopt a certain standard of living that was comfortable but not in any way lavish. Then they promised God that anything above and beyond that would be given away to resource missions. A number of highly successful years later that couple are now very wealthy indeed, but have stuck to their covenant, and consequently very large sums of money have been given away from the profits of their company into missions.

Ceiling standards do two things: they firstly protect your own heart and mind from the insidious infection of materialism and keep you in the driving seat of your resources. Secondly, they release resources to those in desperate need.

Impulse fast

Much money is spent by large corporations to discover what will persuade potential customers to feel dissatisfied with their lives and thus create a desire to 'impulsively' buy their product. Good 'body armour' to protect from this weapon of deceit is a fast from 'impulse buying.' A friend of mine who has a very comfortable lifestyle and was very used to buying clothes on impulse felt challenged by God to not buy any clothes for one year. Her story is a challenging one as she describes 'withdrawal' in terms not dissimilar to more familiar addictions. Having travelled that 365-day fast she is now largely free from the 'indoctrination of impulse' and able to use more of her resources for the battle.

I struggle with impulsiveness particularly where a 'bargain' is concerned. I have often come home having purchased something, and my wife will ask me that provocative question 'Why did you buy that?' To which I reply pathetically, 'It was a bargain.' A bargain isn't a bargain unless you 'need' it, outside of that it is an impulsive waste of money.

Tithing tyrant

I do not have space here to give a full theological critique of this particular aspect of Christian stewardship. Suffice it to say that tithing has been held up as our great goal of giving, yet I believe it totally fails to reflect God's ideal for giving in the context of the New Covenant. If only Salvationists would give 10% of their incomes, our financial situation would be incredibly different. The days of the public paying to keep our corps halls open, lit and warm, are a calendar of shame within our denominational history. In many places miserly giving by soldiers has meant valuable resources, generously given by the public, have not been used how they should. It is true to say that giving is one of the most accurate spiritual thermometers (see Endnote 1, p. 116).

All of this said, the emphasis of Scripture seems to be that God is concerned **not so much about what we give but rather what we keep** (Luke 21:3–4). If the earth is the Lord's and everything in it, then all that we have is purely on loan. Therefore the question of giving focuses more upon what we are allowed to keep. I believe that the 10% refered to in the Old Testament was more a limit upon what we could spend on personal self-indulgence. The rest was designed to be used for the work of God. (See Tony Campolo – *The Kingdom of God is a Party* [published by Nelson Word] for a fuller discussion on this issue.)

Whatever we believe about tithing, it cannot be allowed to cage us into starving God's work of the essential resources needed. My simple suggestion is to make 10% your first target of giving but then seek to simplify your lifestyle over the following months in such a way as to make 15% available and so on. Your financial life then becomes an exciting journey of giving, and seeking to make increasing amounts of money available. I know of a couple who one year gave away 37% of their disposable income and blessed many people through this (see Endnote 2, p. 116).

Inevitably circumstances change and so giving levels will alter in light of these, but again it puts you and not the advertisers in the driving seat of your resources, which is essential for any serious warrior.

What to Buy

Having talked about our need to live counter to the consumerist culture it is important to think about what we actually spend our money upon. What follows are questions that can be asked to help us 'spend well.'

Luxury tax

If we are to buy a luxury item it may be good to impose some kind of luxury tax upon yourself to share those 'spare' resources. If you are spending £500 on an item, impose a tax of say £100 and send that to an appropriate cause. The imposition of this tax will help you avoid significant waste.

Has it been produced ethically?

Many items in our shops have been produced at the expense of third-world labourers and are heavily tainted with unethical working practices. It is true to say that most items would be tainted in one form or another but this must not 'fossilise' us into inactivity. Most nations have a 'fair trading' council. Get some information from yours.

Can I share it?

The rank individualism of our society has propagated a selfishness that is destroying any sense of community in many places. The New Testament Church had an incredible impact upon its culture in that many things were held 'in common' and were available for people who had needs (Acts 2:42–47; 4:32–37). It lived out a form of 'commonism,' where all things belonged to God and were held 'in trust' for the use of the community. Private ownership was not disavowed, but rather subjugated for the needs of others within their relational network.

There is a corps in which a number of people share a lawnmower. In the same church a number of people who use public transport for work have insured their cars for others within the community, to use during the day. These are just small things, but are indicative of the kind of 'community ownership' focus that can be used to again stand against the spirit of the age, as well as releasing resources.

Can I recycle it?

Whether it be aluminium cans or clothes, an 'eco-friendly' lifestyle of preservation rather than blind consumption, immediately puts you in the 'part of the answer' bracket. There is little point in striving to redeem a world if by our very lifestyle we are working against such an agenda.

At its heart, prophetic simplicity is self-renunciation for the cause of Christ. None of the preceding points should be viewed as legalistic, though they could easily become so. No, these are weapons of grace. Choices made in grace, under grace and for grace, are empowered by the God of grace. Scripture teaches:

> *'Above all else, guard your heart, for it is the wellspring of life.'* (Proverbs 4:23)

Consequently the battle for it must be unrelenting. We must be ever-vigilant to areas of vulnerability never allowing it to be captured by the enemies of our soul.

Cupid and the Compromise Conspiracy

I once sat in a Salvation Army meeting and listened as a retired officer told the story of a woman he met 50 years ago. Like himself, she was a Salvationist, deeply committed to God and his purposes for her life. Between the two sprang up a deep affection. However, at the same time, it became increasingly clear that God was calling them in separate directions.

After much heartache, tears and prayer they realised that, although they were deeply in love and very much wanted to be married, God had called them to run different races. Consequently their relationship had to end. He was called to Salvation Army officership and she to serve in her existing profession. Same commitment, different callings. The hurt and pain was significant, yet they both knew that the call of God upon their lives was more important than their romantic desires.

Faithfully they both served God for the next ten years within the fields to which they had been called, only to be overwhelmed by joy when the living God called that same woman into Salvation Army officership. This she obeyed and subsequently married the man she had continued to love during those years. The couple then went on to enjoy 30 years of happy marriage in the service of their King.

I sat deeply moved by this story. All in the congregation were challenged by the officer's commitment (his wife had recently died). We learnt two important lessons that every good warrior needs to learn. Firstly, God's call has to be the primary focus of our lives. Secondly, warriors need more than love to have an effective and appropriate marriage.

I can't live...

The pop song of the 70s poured it out: 'I can't live, if living is without you. I can't live, I can't give anymore.' Emotions stirred and expectations were manipulated. Yet any warrior with any sense wants to cry out 'Rubbish!' It is a tragedy that the myths of the romance market, often propagated by the music world and publications that pour out this literary drivel have become the operating principle for many people's lives.

I meet so many Salvationists, young and old, who have swallowed these destructive myths and plot their lives around finding Mr or Miss Right. Even worse, their perception of the elusive 'right' person has been defined by Hollywood rather than the values of the Kingdom of God. This has stunted the spiritual growth of some, shipwrecked the lives of others. How should a warrior view the issue of romantic relationships?

What is this thing called 'love'?

Before suggesting one or two principles for helping to navigate the high seas of love I want to challenge some of the populist perspectives on these issues. Firstly, love itself. The Beatles sang to us 'All you need is love' and could not have been more wrong. Love is a commitment, not a feeling. Love is as much a decision of the will as it is a 'flutter' of the heart. If the only thing holding a couple together is their hormonal and romantic encounters, then that relationship is doomed. Love is about covenant, a 'no matter what' breed of commitment.

Many missionaries of the past and present came together out of a commitment to a common vision and desire for companionship, then went on to develop a wonderful and deep loving relationship. We are told consistently that 'love' must come first and the rest is worked on later. Tragically the history of the contemporary Army and Church is littered with the casualties of decisions made about long-term commitment, and relationships based predominantly on romance. For any serious warrior there is always a higher call. The choice of the life partner is much more than an issue of relational commitment and involvement. Just because someone is a Christian doesn't make it right to marry them. I want to suggest that the following principles must therefore be considered.

Principles of love

All that follows are obviously ideals, yet it is with them we must begin in order to map out the most effective way forward in our individual situations.

The call of God is primary

The couple mentioned earlier had committed themselves to follow Christ. Hebrews 12:3 tells us that we must *'run with perseverance the race marked out for us.'* This couple recognised that initially God had called them to run a different race. Love on its own is rarely enough for serious warriors to give themselves to each other in marriage. The couple ideally should **double, rather than halve, their usefulness to the Kingdom by their relationship**. If, by coming together, their effectiveness in the war may be jeopardised, then the relationship must be seriously up for question. This is not as harsh and cold as it sounds. The Western world has fed its citizens the Hollywood myth without restraint. Simultaneously, it has witnessed the greatest breakdown in human relationships and family life in all of history. Individual choice, freedom and satisfaction have destroyed relational commitment and made a mockery of the concept of covenant love.

Be as clear about your dreams and visions as possible. In many of our negative cultures the idea of dreaming dreams is discouraged, yet it is something that Scripture actively encourages. Having a perspective upon what God has called you to will be very helpful in shaping relational decisions. In many senses it is a starting point for consideration. I often suggest to people who are focused on being totally God's man or woman, to set up a kind of qualification template into which someone must be able to fit if they are to be considered in the dating option. For example, a person needs to have a similar vision and commitment to God, have an ownership of commitment to the church/movement they are part of, have common values as to physical expression of intimacy outside of marriage and share some of your similar values and ideals. The challenge then is to have a Christian friend you trust to call you to account when Cupid has done his work.

Some may say that this is all too mechanical. Surely a Christian couple can trust God to help them make these types of decisions and don't need this kind of legalistic cage. Perhaps they can, yet my experience of working with people over the years is that they find it very difficult to discern the difference between the Holy Spirit and their hormones. Anything that can assist us in making good decisions and protecting ourselves and others from terrible hurt must be worth considering. At the end of the day our responsibility is to partner with fellow warriors, irrespective of Hollywood's dreams. I recently heard of a young couple who invited friends they trusted in their church to interview them both, pray with them and call them to account with regards to the love they have for one another. They were determined to have God's best for their lives, irrespective of their feelings for one another which were quite deep, and they knew they had to protect what God had entrusted to them, so they refused to compromise on their ideals.

This may be quite painful reading for those who are already in relationships that they know are wrong and not of God. There is a feeling of being trapped, real fear at the thought of causing a great deal of hurt and guilt at missing God's best for your life. For those in such a situation the old maxim of 'better now than later' may be that which you need to hear. Sometimes the most loving thing we can do is initially the most painful, but for the sake of both parties, and the affairs of the war, it may be the time for the line to be drawn under this particular relationship, while trusting God for the consequences.

Handling Holy Hormones

For those dating, there comes the inevitable tension of how to appropriately express physical intimacy in a way that honours Christ and safeguards the integrity of the relationship. Space does not allow a full commentary upon this issue and consequently I would refer you to some of the resources mentioned in the appendix.

The Sunday School song states: 'This I know, for the

Bible tells me so.' The problem is that with this particular issue of 'how far to go' it doesn't. Certainly the Bible makes clear from even the creation mandate that sexual inter- course was to be a celebration of marriage rather than part of the preparation for it (Genesis 2:24). Yet it is less clear on what is appropriate and helpful before that point. This is reflected in the very common absence of such teaching in holiness meetings and even youth group environments. This said, I do not believe Scripture leaves us blind on the issue, and I offer the following for reflection on this crucial subject.

'No hints . . .'

The apostle Paul tells it straight to the Ephesian church by calling them to be 'imitators of God.' By definition this means having 'not even a hint of sexual immorality, or of any kind of impurity' (Ephesians 5:1–3). In many Western cultures where sexually explicit language and behaviour are propagated as the norm, the warrior must be vigilant that temptation does not take them down the same route, nor even give the impression that they are doing so. It is not that God thinks that physical and hormonal drives are wrong; after all he invented them. Rather, the Bible teaches that they should be expressed in the right environment.

R.E.S.P.E.C.T.

This Aretha Franklin song asked a fundamental question that runs as a constant theme throughout Scripture: that of respecting human-kind who are created in the image of God. Peter calls for this to be worked out very practically in our everyday lives (1 Peter 2:17), and I believe it is key to physical expression within relationships. Whether it be in a married or pre-marital context, respect is to undergird all our relationships. Consequently what we do physically within them must be driven by this attitude of respect, ensuring that the levels of intimacy expressed fall in line with this.

Additionally we need to 'respect' our varying levels of

self-control if we are not to miss God's best. The point where individual couples draw the line may well be different, but the principle of keeping as far away from the 'danger' zones as possible is a wise and helpful one. Returning to the war analogy, one of the greatest threats to human life are the minefields, particularly when no maps or boundaries are marked. Only a fool walks close to the area where they think the edge is. The wise will keep well clear of the whole area.

'In his steps ...'

This classic book by Charles Sheldon records the story of a group of people who committed themselves to live out their contemporary lives by first asking: 'What would Jesus do in my situation?' Thought simplistic by many, the story records the challenges and hardships faced by people making this kind of commitment. I have personally been called naive when encouraging people to apply this principle to relationships, yet would ask that it be considered by readers. Simplistic, maybe. A cure-all, sadly not. A good check and balance, definitely.

Our sexual being and integrity is precious and valuable, and it needs protecting and looking after. This will require discipline, commitment and some strong guidelines. Again, I refer you to the material listed in the appendix. I have given space to this subject because so many of the singles and dating couples I meet regularly struggle to honour God in this area. I have met many who at one time hungered to serve God in their warrior role, yet because they failed in this particular arena, now find themselves a long way from the battle front. This is such a crucial area and I feel the Church has often failed to give the teaching and encouragement we need. In the battle for the heart, this is one of the fiercest that must be won.

But what if ...?

The reality for many is that they have already failed in this arena and they could read the above as dismissing them from the war. Nothing could be further from the truth. Our God is a God of new beginnings and loves to restore weak, fallen people like me and you. He specialises in turning the apparently-unresolvable into the renewed and revived. He certainly can't give us back our virginity but he can give us our purity, which, really in one sense, is what virginity is all about. For those who have gone through the agony of divorce, the 'decree absolute' relates to your marital status not to your usefulness to God in the field of battle. In one sense, those who have been wounded are more qualified in helping those in current pain. There is no such thing as a lost cause or being 'beyond the point of no return' in the Kingdom of God: just a group of very grateful, forgiven people. Living in the freedom of that fact/position is also an important battle to be won.

Singleness

The twelfth commandment?

Moses was given the first 10, Jesus added another one (John 13:34–35) and tragically the Church has invented a new one all of its own – **'Thou shalt be married.'**

If we were to pause and listen to this unwritten, but very clear rule the church often gives out, we would hear that it is somehow odd not to be wed. Those who choose, or are called to a life of celibacy, or those who are single for want of a suitable partner, are often made to feel second-class and not quite 'normal.' I have even heard of people barred from leadership because they aren't married. This is justified by ripping scriptural verses out of their context and doing significant violence to the text in the process. Unfortunately, this cuts out the apostle Paul and even the incarnate Son of God himself. In light of such unbiblical nonsense, this attitude needs a serious rethink.

When writing this section I asked for the input of a friend who is single. He shared quite honestly about the struggles he has faced:

- Not being treated as 'normal.'
- Rarely being invited out as a single person.
- Going for weeks without any physical intimacy with another human being.
- Who would notice if he died?
- How long would it take to be discovered?

This issue needs to be addressed by churches and corps if we are just to express basic Christian community as well as being the platform for these warriors to fight effectively.

The apostle Paul challenges us to lift up the value of singleness (1 Corinthians 7:8), and see it as a significant weapon in the armoury of the Church of God. We need to affirm singleness, and facilitate a community that includes rather than excludes those on that path. They are free to go to places married and family types find it difficult to go to. They can focus much more on the task in hand with no distraction to divert their ministry. A whole rethink is needed not only in our attitude, but in church and corps life practice, that will release these warriors with all the encouragement and affirmation that Scripture accords.

Don't wait

I have lost count of the number of single men and women that I have met who are just waiting around for that Mills and Boon moment. The moment when that knight or knightess will come along in shining 'navy serge' and sweep them off of their feet, riding off with them into the sunset. They have tragically swallowed this myth, imposed upon them by their society and church, that happiness and fulfilment can only be found in partnership with someone else. The net result of this is many frustrated people languishing in the mire of this cultural and felt-need swamp, longing for that moment to arrive. Yet it does not have to be this way.

Singleness is not about waiting, but rather living life to the full in the service of God. That's easy for you, some may say. You are married. Married I am, but I do have a pair of ears and have heard the many testimonies of people who are hungering after the abundant life (John 10:10) that Christ promised in the service of him and his world. Can there have been a more fulfilled person than Jesus, or saintly Mother Theresa, and thousands of others who have walked this path of discipleship and warrior lifestyle?

None of this is to deny the frustrations that may be involved with these issues, and I do not wish to be insensitive to people wrestling with such, yet let us remind ourselves again: 'We are at war.' When on a war footing extreme measures of sacrifice and service are required. This may mean singleness for some, financial down-sizing and simplicity for others. The sacrifice of nations who are at war on a corporate level, and that demonstrated by individuals, shows us something of the kind of things that will be required in this war. I caught a glimpse of the nature of 'wartime' decisions with the feared death of my daughter. If we are to take our warfare and military metaphors seriously, the above issues must be faced and victory achieved.

Endnotes

1. This is not a slight on hardworking officers who often work beyond the call of duty in serving corps and communities in challenging circumstances. The reality is that many who give to us may not object too strongly to paying for a Salvation Army presence within their community. This though cannot be an excuse for local Salvationists not taking responsibility for their own corps programme and worshipping facilities. Our personal giving **must** reflect our commitment to the vision and mission within our locality that we want to be known for.

2. This demonstrates our need for wealthy warriors who will invest effectively to release much needed resources. It is a challenge to all of us in the privileged nations to live appropriately and prophetically in relation to our resources.

Chapter 4

Battle for the Will

Choosing what a warrior should choose

The young monk sat outside the ecclesiastical court, his heart and mind racing at a pace. Was he crazy? What did he think he was doing? The church had made him what he was. They had invested in him, provided him with opportunity to do all that he felt God required of him. They provided for his upkeep, food, clothing. His standing in the community, in truth much of his self-esteem and identity, his reputation and his entire future came from the hands of the people he was about to see; and they were none too pleased. At the end of the meeting everything that had ever been important to him, including, some might suggest, his life itself, could be taken from him.

It had all begun with an aching hunger that grew within him. An angst, a mental and spiritual disquiet that would not go away. It gnawed at the very core of his being and raised questions that demanded to be answered. He had never meant to walk down this theological and now very political path; it seemed almost to happen by chance. Many times he had fought a mental duel with himself, his will, beliefs and fear all pitched in battle. He had laid on the simple bed in his sparse chamber agonising over this journey of faith and obedience.

The scales seemed to be continually tipping from side to side. On one side was the almost ridiculous conviction that he had discovered biblical truth; apparently it 'appeared hidden' from the sight of the common people by the ecclesiastical authorities. This truth provided the means of liberation from the tyranny of a faith that could never be adequately fulfilled, the very essence of a system which set you up for perpetual failure other than through slavish obedience to the system of which he was a part. From his own experience, this still left you cold and unsure as to your standing in Christ; it didn't answer the cry of your soul. Yet what he had discovered, what had come to life on the pages of the manuscripts he knew so well, had ignited within him a fire whose embers burned with ever-increasing intensity, irrespective of the cold water of fear that continually poured over them.

On the other side was the church, the state, the ecclesiastical hierarchy, some of his friends and even his own sense of loyalty that stood as a counterpoint to this challenge. What arrogance, what insane lunacy had taken hold of him to challenge hundreds of years of tradition? As far as he knew, no one had ever challenged it, even dared to question the mighty authority of the Roman church. He had heard rumours of those that had asked other questions and the word was that they had been summarily dealt with, with very few questions asked. Yet here he was, this monk of little repute pitting himself in conflict against the amassed powers of the ecclesiastical world.

Yet what came continually to his mind, the balance in his decision, was his fresh assurance of the grace of God, demonstrated by the love of Christ, ignited by the power of the Holy Spirit that had consumed his sinful, but now forgiven and grateful heart. The warmth of this new encounter that had revolutionised his mind and spirit and had brought freedom to his sin-sick soul, now massaged his frightened heart as he stood to walk into the court that would seal his future.

As he entered heads turned, whispers were exchanged, and there were many looks of disdain upon the faces of the assembled might of his clerical world. His heart pounded in his heaving chest. He caught only some of the accusations being hurled at him. The detail was irrelevant, the charge of theological treachery called heresy was crystal clear. His attention flipped between his accuser and his doubts; they seemed to swarm around him, buzzing like angry bees. Images, pictures of his childhood, his ordination, his reading Scripture late into the night, illumined by the mystical flicker of a candle, his friends warnings, his own theological wrestling, fear for the future of his physical well-being; all these cut into his attention on the statements being made.

Suddenly the words being uttered brought clarity to his mental wanderings. The word 'Recant' with its unuttered yet very real threat of terminal consequences, focused his mind. The intensity of anger and frustration filled the room with an almost tangible cloak of intimidation and aggression. Silence fell upon the room as an answer was awaited. The young monk stood, choked with fear, unable to utter a response. The demand to 'recant' was repeated, increasingly in its forcefulness and intention. He bowed to the floor, praying for courage, and drew a deep breath; the silence was deafening. Then, as he constructed his response, the only one he knew he could give, the power of the Spirit of God fused with his will, banishing his fear. With his voice freed he announced his response, the words and consequences of which have been heard and felt around the world for generations. With his life on the line he proclaimed, 'Here I stand. I can do no other, so help me God.'

On that day the reformation of the Church and the world began. On that day Martin Luther won the battle for his will.

Today, Yesterday and Forever!

It is unlikely that many of us would often face the challenges encountered by Martin Luther as he took on the might of the Roman Church, and became the catalyst for the world-changing Reformation. This said, he faced an issue that has been common to all humankind since the time of Adam and Eve up to the present: the battle of the will. The choice between 'self-will' and 'God's will' is ever before us and is the final battle that must be won. Irrespective of how long we have followed Christ this will be an continual fight against our own nature. In the book of Romans the apostle Paul speaks of his constant struggle against his own 'selfish desires' to do what he knows is right.

'We know that the law is spiritual; but I am unspiritual, sold as a slave to sin. I do not understand what I do. For what I want to do I do not do, but what I hate I do. And if I do what I do not want to do, I agree that the law is good . . . For I have the desire to do what is good, but I cannot carry it out. For what I do is not the good I want to do; no, the evil I do not want to do – this I keep on doing . . . So I find this law at work: When I want to do good, evil is right there with me.'   (Romans 7:14–21)

This internal wrestling of which Paul spoke and with which Luther struggled, is at the heart of our war. Failure in this engagement will at best limit our effectiveness, at worst it will nullify us. As spirit-filled people there is still a battle to be won. In military terms the enemy of our souls will not give up one inch of territory to our obedience; every part will be contested, nothing will be surrendered. What follows are some of the challenges and strategies involved in this battle of the will.

'I submit'

Many of us have been born in a culture that resists the concept of submitting to anything or anyone. Yet the key to effective and victorious Christian living is an active choice to submit to God. Much is said in the modern world about the desire for freedom, and some turn away from the Christian faith, declaring it merely to be a tool of captivity and control. The truth is that everyone is a slave to something or someone, the only question being whether that something or someone is an appropriate master for us. Whether it be God, money, fashion or the expectations of others, we all have a master. **True freedom is not the absence of slavery but the presence of the right master**. Part of the paradox of the Christian faith is that the more we surrender to God, the more we are freed to be who we are meant to be. It is in our voluntary slavery that we find ultimate freedom. As Milton wrote in *Paradise Lost*:

'Freely we serve because we freely love.' [45]

The apostle Paul again highlights the truth of this for us.

> *'But now that you have been set free from sin and have become slaves to God, the benefit you reap leads to holiness, and the result is eternal life.'* (Romans 6:22)

Paul had different words he could have used in this passage, one referring to a servant or the other being that of a slave. He chose consistently to use the unpaid, no rights image of the slave, to demonstrate his perspective on following Christ.

Despite the truth of this, we still all face the inner battle that the apostle Paul so clearly articulated. Part of the development of the church in recent years has been a very much needed move away from legalism and duty, and a move towards freedom in Christ. Yet I fear in many places this has just mirrored the cry of our individualistic and self-centred culture. This has meant a freedom from so much of what commitment to Christ is meant to be, and an enslavement to the god of comfort that our society worships. This is just cheap grace. It is grace abused. It is grace prostituted for our own desires. We are called to a life of complete surrender to Christ. Keith Green was crystal clear and exactly right:

> 'Lord kill me, destroy me, burn me beyond recognition with your holiness – I know that you would never hurt or harm me. You only want me dead! Let it be done!' [46]

The battles for the heart and mind are lost and won in the battle for the will. To say we believe and are soldiers of Jesus Christ, whilst refusing to submit, is to not believe. The submission of the will is an absolute for the serious warrior. Dietrich Bonhoefer stated clearly:

> 'When Christ calls a man, he bids him to come and die.' [47]

This is an issue of life and death, it is only in dying that you truly can live. The 'old man' of your pre-Christian days must be executed, with no leniency, and no mercy given. The monastic aesthetics used to go to extreme ends to purge themselves of 'self'. Whilst wanting to avoid the excesses of personal flaying and physical abuse it is important that we take the battle seriously. There can be no clemency, no amnesty given to the old man within you, he has to be crucified. We cannot afford no-go areas of our lives, no matter how hard it may be.

So often believers struggle with faith without realising it is in submitting that victory is to be found. It is as we surrender our will to his will that we are able to receive the full empowerment of the Spirit (Ephesians 1:13) and live an effective warrior lifestyle. The devotion of total surrender opens the doorway to blessing and empowerment.

One of the most challenging songs I know is 'All to Jesus I surrender, all to him I freely give.'[48] The battle for the will begins in a decision to walk this path. When using this song I often ask people not to sing if they do not believe it to be true within their lives. Part of me expects absolute silence at that point; Christians may not often tell lies but they regularly sing them. The challenge of this song is uncompromising yet needs to be fully embraced in the will.

'One for You, Two for Me'

The reality for many of us is a compartmentalised commitment. A commitment which sees areas of our lives fully surrendered and others still very much our own property. My mother used to have a money box containing all our weekly finances. This was divided up with movable partitions, holding different aspects of the budget: food, clothes, gas and electricity. We too easily compartmentalise our lives, allowing God only limited access to particular areas. This results in a diffused focus and limits the impact of our lives upon the world. This is primarily an issue of obedience. I meet many would-be warriors who wrestle with holding onto areas of their lives that need to be surrendered to God. The dividers need pulling out providing a surrendered whole.

It is interesting that James closely links his instruction to *'submit'* with his advice to *'resist the devil, and he will flee from you'* (James 4:7). It is in the submission to the ways of God that we are most equipped and enabled to resist the devil, limiting the areas of weakness for him to attack. The most vulnerable areas on a field of battle are those that have not been secured, or have been left unguarded due to over-confidence. Areas of our lives that are unsurrendered provide significant gaps in our armour, leaving us most vulnerable to attack. The film *Independence Day* climaxes (like so many similar films) in the heroes finding the one weakness in the protective force field of the invading aliens. What is true in the fantasy world of Hollywood is also found to be true in our spiritual battle. Surrender is the 'force field' of protection that we have.

In corps and churches one of the most effective weapons in the hands of the enemy is a believer with a will that is divided by unsurrendered areas of their life. This can range from wealthy people keeping too much of their God-given resources to themselves, causing hardship in the lives of those without in their fellowship, to others who carry a bitter and critical spirit in their relationships and dealings with others. Such areas of life are the most fertile of soils for division and compromise. The early Army was fully aware of this strategy of Satan.

'He has succeeded first, in deceiving them as to the standard of their own religious life ... He has got them to lower the standard which Jesus Christ himself established in his book – a standard, not only aimed at, but to be attained unto – a standard of victory over sin, the world, the flesh, and the devil. Real, living, reigning, triumphing Christianity!' [49]

Submission is not so much a one-off decision of the will but rather it is cultivated by the habit of obedience forged on the anvil of discipline.

Discipline

This is not one of the most popular terms in our modern day, but it is fundamental in winning the battle for the will. It is the heart of discipleship and effective warfare. Historically, whenever a large Army has been defeated by a much smaller force, the difference has nearly always been the contrast in discipline. In Christ's time, the dominance of the Roman nation was founded upon the discipline of the Roman legions. So it is with a soldier of Jesus Christ. Discipline is essential.

Back in 1991 there was an American yachtsman by the name of Michael Plant, known as one of the world's finest yachtsman. He had circumnavigated the globe in solo voyages three times and was about the take part in the BOC race, a solo competition around the world. Plant had just taken delivery of a new boat, a *Coyote*. He was sailing it from New York City harbour across the north Atlantic to France where the BOC race was to begin.

Each day, the support crew would talk to him by radio-satellite. On the ninth day they lost contact with Plant. This worried no one – there were storms over the Atlantic and they presumed he was busy. However, after six days of radio silence his support crew began to get anxious. On the seventh day, they launched a full-scale international rescue operation. All the planes going back across the Atlantic were told to listen for radio signals and every ship in the area was alerted. After two weeks, the *Coyote* was found, 450 miles south west of Ireland, floating upside down. Michael Plant's body has never been discovered.

When the *Coyote* was pulled out of the water it was discovered that the keel of the boat had sheared totally away. What had originally been an 8000-pound weight beneath the boat had disappeared. To this day no one knows how that happened. Whether there was a defect in the manufacture of the boat or whether it hit an undersea obstacle or submarine, no one has any idea. Some kind of catastrophic moment happened when the weight below the waterline became lighter than the weight above the waterline.

As I read this story about the *Coyote* and Michael Plant's terrible accident, I realised this made a vivid illustration for our own Christian lives. The whole principle on which a yacht operates is that the weight **below** the waterline is far heavier than the deck, rigging, designer technology and sails **above** the sea level. If, that weight is lost or un-balanced, as was the case with Michael Plant, the yacht is left vulnerable, likely to capsize at the first sign of trouble. So in the Christian life the real work of the man and woman desiring to be a person of God is not what is built **above** the waterline but **below** it. (This story appears in *The Life God Blesses* by Gordon MacDonald.)

Building the keel

Discipline is that which sets apart the Christian 'wanderer' from the Christian 'warrior.' The wanderer is the type of person that promises the world but never produces the goods. They spend their lives praising God that they are no longer the person they once were, but never become the person that God saved them to be. They jump from one commitment to another, responding at every and any opportunity – all dependent upon the passion of the preacher or the intensity of the moment. They normally come forward at a point in an appeal when it is most noticeable (normally after about the twelfth repetition of the appeal song) and commit themselves again to the 'new thing God is calling them to.' The tragedy of these people is not their lack of sincerity, that is not in question, but rather that their life is a series of disappointments and frustrations, of never sticking to anything of worth.

These people are in desperate need of what a friend of mine calls post-encounter endurance. The only route to this endurance is the development of discipline. This is not about legalism but rather the achievement of goals. Disciplines can easily become 'legalisms' if they become ends in themselves rather than means to an end. However, when properly applied they provide the platform upon which achievements of true substance can be built and developed.

Captain Sandra Ryan in her teaching on discipleship likens this tension to learning to play the piano. The discipline of playing scales and arpeggios initially seemed like legalistic repetition to her. Yet it was only after some years of doing this, that she was able to sit down and play more or less anything that was put in front of her. Discipline enabled her playing to become a lot closer to that of her favourite composer, Chopin. The same is true for Christians. Without developing certain disciplines we stand little or no chance of behaving anything like Jesus.

Self-discipline is developed and worked out in different ways, producing diverse aspects of lifestyle and character. At its heart, it is an intention that directs lifestyle and life choices towards a predetermined goal of bringing the best of who we are to the forefront of battle. Following are some of the different forms of disciplines and their related outcomes:

- **Chastity** – This builds healthy relationships. Not just a physical chastity within existing male/female relationships, but a chastity which rejects self-centred relationships that seek pure self-fulfilment and give nothing.
- **Bible study/Christian reading** – This builds faith and knowledge. The word of God is given as *'a lamp unto our feet and a light unto our path.'* Reading of how God has dealt with and used his people in the past is an essential foundational discipline. Also reading biographies of the saints past and present is most helpful in shaping our wills.
- **Prayer** – This protects ourselves and others. It also develops our holiness and relationship with God which in turn shapes so much of our relationships

with others. The popular usage of the term 'spiritual warfare' comes within this discipline. I have not dealt with this specifically as our effectiveness within this realm of warfare is almost entirely dependent upon us winning the personal battles we address within this book. A life of constant defeat in lifestyle will be the same in prayer.

- **Fasting** – This again develops our relationship with God as well as bringing our will and appetites into subjection to our will. I have personally struggled continually with this, for I know that if I cannot win a personal battle at this most basic level, the much greater victories will be far from my grasp.

- **Fellowship** – The building of healthy and mutually supportive relationships is obviously essential. This can easily get lost in a busy life, but the reality is that these relationships are built only with regular doses of time. As well as strengthening corps life and providing a 'warm and welcoming environment' for new people, there are numerous personal fruits. For those of us possessed by the 'programme demon' we need to work hard at this aspect of discipline.

- **Solitude** – The coming apart from people and business is essential for regaining perspective and for reflection and prayer. It brings back balance and focus, giving God 'space' to speak into our cluttered lives. Our faces may not glow like that of Moses, but we will be transformed by the experience.

- **Giving/simplicity** – We have already spoken in depth on this subject, but here it is reiterated as a discipline. It breaks our dependency on things and develops greater trust in God. This benefits ourselves as much as those to whom we may give.

- **Worship** – This builds relationship with God, as well as community within a church. I fear for those of us brought up in a church where corporate and personal worship has become a formal exercise, rather than an intimate encounter.

- **Rest** – This keeps us alive and effective. Those who work with me may laugh that I have the audacity to include something at which I am so bad. It is true that I do have problems with the concepts of 'eight-hour days,' 'five-day weeks' and 'retirement.' Yet is essential that soldiers do occasionally get relieved to enable them to recharge their batteries. As the old adage goes, 'We are called not to burn out, but to burn on.'

- **Celebration** – Our lives are designed to express the foretaste of the great homecoming for all nations to the banqueting table of God. This being so, celebration needs to be at the very heart of who we are. Even though we find ourselves in the midst of war we must celebrate the victory that is ours in Christ, and we must seek to live out the life abundant (John 10:10) that Jesus called us to and that his life, death and resurrection makes possible.

It is vital that warriors develop a lifestyle that incorporates these aspects of discipline so that we might battle well. Those disciplines we find hardest, or which do not come naturally, must be mastered if we are to be most effective.

Willing to Choose

Choice is at the very core of the battle for our will. In particular those things we 'choose' to allow to be part of us are important in honing our wills. Our mind and will must be an area that can be impacted by the hurts and struggles of the world around us. Living as many of us do in the fast-moving soundbite culture, it is easy to stand aloof and detached from the reality of the world around us. A relatively new term has been incorporated into the Western vocabulary: 'compassion fatigue.' In the wake of Romanian orphanages, the Rwandan, Zairean and Bosnian wars, it has become an acceptable norm for us to observe tremendous tragedy and just switch off. Whether we do it literally with our TV sets, or just emotionally, our coping mechanism easily leads us to cold-heartedness, hopeless-ness or cynicism. The effective warrior must resist this, so that we might develop that strong yet tender heart that is able to 'weep with those who weep.' This is a continual challenge to me and a lesson that became tangible and powerful for me during a visit to Russia.

We were being shown around a hospital that cared for survivors of the blockade of Leningrad (St. Petersburg). We entered a room where there were four elderly ladies, one of whom told us her story. She had seen most of her extended family slaughtered by the Nazis in one day. Over the next year she also witnessed the death of her husband and eldest son. One of her other children starved to death and the remaining child just managed to survive through being breastfed but she was so ill that after the war she retired from work early due to consistent ill health.

The story was deeply moving for all of us in the room and obviously evoked painful memories for the others there, as tears began to be shed in abundance. As it was time for us to go, I went round to say goodbye, kissing each old lady on the cheek as I went. As I approached the lady who had told her story, I bent down to kiss her. As I did so a tear that was running down her cheek caught my own and began to run down my face. I froze, goose bumps came up all over my back, and I was just about to wipe it away when I heard or sensed God say, 'Leave it alone, Phil Wall. For once in your life feel something of the pain others do.'

I tell the story to illustrate the all-important point. It is too easy for us to turn off the TV, put away the newspaper, walk by on the other side of the road, as an anaesthetic to the pain of others. Yet a warrior must embrace it, allow it to become part of who he or she is as they seek to share something of God's heart of compassion for the world. We must reject crippling cynicism and 'pain avoidance.' It is part of the package; their pain must become, in part, our pain. Pity cries and says, 'That's a shame.' Compassion weeps and says, 'I'll help.'

Where and What?

Choices made within the will very much determine how we live day by day. Not only do we need to allow issues close to God's heart to impact our lives, we also need to make the decisions that will shape the lives we live. Where we live and what we do are two of the most important.

Our patch

The history of the people of God is littered with the importance of geography. From the specifics of the promised land to the precise command of Jesus relating to Jerusalem, Judea, Samaria and the ends of the earth, geography has been important. Tragically this has been lost in many places and it may be one of those things that need to be rediscovered.

In my own corps we have sought to develop something of a 'gangland mentality' for our area. To the people it is our community, what happens to them happens to us, what concerns them concerns us. To the powers of darkness this is our place and we declare war on the minions of the 'god of this world'. We are going to take this area for our King and secure this as a stronghold of the Kingdom.

In our prayers we carry a burden and a passion for our area, we immerse ourselves in its heart and atmosphere, we make its issues our issues. It is a reflection of the incarnational principle of Christ himself. The apostle John records that *'The Word became flesh and made his dwelling among us'* (John 1:14), which literally translated means 'he pitched his tent among us.' Ultimately he paid the consequences for such identification on the cross and we seek to live out similar lives. We ask God for his concern for this community and seek his wisdom in identifying the strategic 'keys' for unlocking the area to the gospel.

In real terms this is the difference between many Roman Catholic and Protestant missionaries I have observed in visits to the third world. Many, though not all, of the Protestant missionaries live in a kind of 'ex-pat' fortress with all the comforts of home in terms of luxury items, food, housing etc. Their actual engagement with the indigenous community is purely on a professional commuting level. They leave the security of the 'compound' in the morning, **do** their mission stuff, and then return to 'little England' or its nationalistic equivalent in the evening. Their values, lifestyles, customs and language remain largely unchanged. Then there are the other types – Roman Catholic and Protestant missionaries who take the incarnation a bit more literally and actually immerse themselves within the indigenous culture. They learn the language, live at the same economic level and seek as best they can to engage with the culture they are seeking to serve.

The most stark version of this I have come across is some Roman Catholic nuns who at risk of death remained in Ethiopia as it was their 'home' and whatever the threat they were not going to leave. Or closer to home, numbers of Army missionaries have sought to engage with the Russian culture in which they are serving, and are paying a price to achieve this in terms of their own safety and welfare. Whatever example we use the principle remains the same. You can only realistically reach a community in which you are immersed and part of. Hit-and-run 'outreach' never has and never will work. We need to fight for an area as we would if we were defending our own homes, our patch.

Intentional Accommodation

Where and how we live is quite important for being most effective in our warfare and the following are some creative options that may intensify the war effort.

Wage share

Many of our corps are filled with individuals living in over-resourced housing that use inappropriate amounts of finance. One way of breaking this cycle is to covenant with others to share and release some of these resources. For example, it is possible for three single people two of them could afford to pay the rent for all three, releasing another from the burden of having to earn wages as such. This could give that person the time to work and serve the people within your community.

House share

I know of a number of churches where it is common practice for families to open up their home and provide accommodation for a young single person, who becomes part of their household and consequently takes some of the responsibility for work in and around the home. Another couple I know took a lone parent and her daughter into their family home and now they are permanent fixtures. This is a strong expression of community in many Western societies that are disintegrating at their heart from lack of tangible community. It can also work the other way, whereby a young person with income offers to move in with a couple who have young children but due to financial pressure are both required to work. This extra income may then release one of the parents to stay at home to provide the primary child care.

The challenge of the cities

The nature of population distribution is dramatically changing. By the year 2000 one half of humanity will be living and working in cities. In 1950 the world had 83 cities with over 1 million inhabitants, at present there are 280 and by the year 2015 there will be more than 500.[50] The make-up of our nations is changing dramatically; the cities will shape much of the future of our world.

Most mission strategists agree that the way to reach the heart of a nation is to win the cities, but tragically recent contemporary Christian history in many places has not helped this goal. In many nations we have witnessed the second exodus of Chrisians away from the urban centres, to the comfort of leafy suburbia. This has had a number of effects in drawing much needed resources from these places but also in leaving the Christians remaining there incredibly isolated. This cannot be the will of God and is something that must change if we are to see our nations won. Many contemporary books and films portray the cities within our future in a violent apocalyptic form. Urban and moral decay running rife and the social fabric literally going rotten. In socio-economic terms it is easy to analyse the reasons behind this, but ultimately when things go rotten it is the responsibility of those who forgot or neglected to put the 'salt' in it.

The strategic nature of the cities make it essential for us to prioritize them in terms of mission, which by definition will mean living there. The old idea of 'commuting' into an urban area to 'do mission' and then leaving to go home has been the scourge of inner-city evangelism for generations. Many Salvation Army corps buildings exist in the inner city but so few, at times if any, of the soldiery live there. This makes effective outreach very difficult and at times the resentments of local people to 'commando' style evangelism is, I feel, often quite vociferous and understandably so. Urban mission can only be fleshed out effectively by those who live there, for only they will have the credibility and the integrity to communicate effectively.

Father Damien was a priest who went to establish a church on a leper colony. Much hard work was done but only a handful of parishioners ever came to church and they were already Christians. Eventually the priest asked to be released from the work due to his total ineffectiveness thus far, but on the day he was leaving, something happened that was to change his destiny and many of those on the island for ever.

As he was getting onto the boat, the sailor saw something on the hands of the priest that made him draw back. The young priest looked at his hands and noticed the white spots of first stage leprosy that had now taken hold of him. The boat left without him and the priest returned to his house knowing that this was to be his home for the rest of his life. News spread fast around the island of the priest who had now become 'one of them', and when he came to open the church for evening mass rather than the handful he had always had, there was a packed congregation. Now he was 'one of them' they were willing to listen.

There is no avoiding this issue. We are going to have to pay the price of living in the cities and to become part of the many disadvantaged and vulnerable communities who live there. That is where the battle is often most fierce and consequently that is where the army of God should be. A preacher friend of mine says that there is never any reason for not living in the city unless God has called us to live and serve elsewhere. The cities and housing estates of our nations need to be our priority.

In many of our cities we have a literal global 'village', on our doorstep. In terms of world mission they need to be reached so they can return to their nations where evangelism is difficult if not illegal. Jesus set his face to the city (Jerusalem) knowing there was a price to be paid to get the job done, ours is a similar call in the war of salvation. A young couple from my corps sensed the 'nudge' of God to a low income housing estate near our hall. When preparing for marriage they bought a flat on the estate, have become part of the residents association, have begun a prayer cell and are at the heart of the growing Christian community there. These are key decisions of the will.

The Call

In addition to our **location**, our **vocation** must be considered as an essential issue of the war. Within The Salvation Army much rhetoric abounds about this particular term which is often confusing and disempowering rather than being the springboard into mission that it should be. Scripture makes it clear in terms of the post-Pentecost Church that all are called and empowered by the Spirit for mission; the only issue is the sphere of the calling. Tragically from about the fourth century on, the Church began to lift up certain forms of ministry in terms of a professional priesthood, thus disempowering the majority of the Church in a change which had a disastrous impact upon the task of world mission.

The divide between a professional priesthood and a so-called non-professional laity is an extra-biblical concept and quite alien to the teaching of Scripture. Rob Frost, the Methodist National Evangelist comments upon this development:

> 'The early Church taught that all members are the *laos* – the people – who have been called out of society to serve God and others. There was to be no hierarchy or different levels of status because all the believers were part of the Church's mission and belong to the people of God. Peter made it clear that everyone is a member of the team when he wrote:
>
> *"But you are a chosen people, a royal priesthood, a holy nation, a people belonging to God, that you may declare the praises of him who called you out of darkness into his wonderful light. Once you were not a people, but now you are the people of God."* [51]   (1 Peter 2:9–10)

Biblically all of us are the *laos*, the people of God, set apart by him to be priests of God.

To allow this professionalising ministry to occur, has surely been one of the most destructive developments in the Church historically as well as in the brief history of our own Movement. The fruit of this transition has been the disempowering of the majority of the Church creating the need for a hybrid form of one-man-band ministry of supposedly multi-gifted individuals. The one-man-band musician is known for his ability to play many instruments at once, but the music he plays is consistently appalling. Visually he is impressive, audibly he is agonising.

Salvation Army doctrine affirms the priesthood of all believers and Colonel Philip Needham comments on the importance of this doctrine of effective mission:

'A dynamic understanding of ministry emphasises the prophetic over the priestly, function over status, mission over maintenance. A Church on the move has more need for leaders who will discern and speak the word of God, than for those who will maintain the traditions. It has no time to create an ecclesiastical hierarchy; ministry must be seen in a functional way as the exercise of Spirit-given gifts for building up the body of Christ (1 Corinthians 12:4ff); that is, for enabling the Church to move forward in its pilgrimage ... The doctrine of the priesthood of all believers, therefore, has a profound affinity to the view of the Church as God's pilgrim people. Privileged priests tend to be a function of static, hierarchical religious institutions. Ministry shared by all and apportioned according to recognised gifts bestowed by the Spirit, tends to be a function of a dynamic community of faith which is ever on the move.' [52]

If we are to see the world won for God, we need to rediscover this theology of calling and ministry. Each called and gifted warrior will need to work it out in their place of influence, fleshing out the gospel for all to see. This is what we say we believe in terms of the priesthood of all believers (1 Peter 2:9). All are priests, all are temples of God's presence (2 Corinthians 6:16) where people can encounter God.

Without this perspective worked out we end up focusing our energies in the wrong direction. A friend of mine, the Rev. Steve Chalke describes it in this way. For centuries we have seen our ministers/officers as the 'front-line' workers who actually do the work, and the rest of the congregation as the 'back-line' workers there to support them in that task. To be honest this has been quite destructive by leaving all the responsibility in the hands of the unfortunate leaders, and everyone else disempowered with little or no ownership of the mission. Yet if we are to take Ephesians 4:11–12 seriously it appears to suggest the exact opposite to be true. The ministers/officers are the back-line workers called and gifted by God to equip the front-line workers for the actual work of ministry. Leader's jobs are to ensure that the church members/soldiers are taught, pastored, trained to evangelise, hear God's prophetic word, and be led (apostled) effectively so that they might do the work out there of being salt and light amongst the unreached masses.

Now of course leaders do get involved on the front line. Where else do they get the experience to train and equip others? Yet their primary focus always needs to be the equipping of the saints for their work. The reality is that they are the ones that work and live alongside those that we are seeking to reach, and consequently need all the encouragement and support they can be given to achieve that task.

If this is in any way a reflection of the real situation, then is it any wonder that we have had some difficulties fulfilling our mandate? If we think the back-line is actually the front-line and the front-line the back, and if the front-line troops think they are the back-line troops and the back-line troops think they are the front-line then we really do have some problems that need thinking and working through! What we need is the back-line people resourcing the front-line so that we resource those on the field of battle to fight and not those back at base camp!

Within our own movement we have fallen prey to this ecclesiastical elitism that has had a very negative impact upon our own work of mission. For Booth, however, the role of an officer was merely a practical tool for releasing more of an individual's time for ministry in the local corps. All Salvationists are gifted, called and commissioned by the Spirit and we desperately need a review of this particular philosophy of ministry if we are to see the effectiveness we dream of.

The power of vocation

This shift in thinking is essential if we are to engage in this war effectively. The greatest shift is for the average

Salvationist to view their role and vocation differently. Their work must be seen as the place of their primary mission. They need to view their workplace as their mission field. Not to recite John 3:16 every two minutes, but that they seek within their role to influence for the Kingdom. Whether in full-time paid employment, working as a house parent, unemployed or retired, the same principle applies. This is the nature of Kingdom theology; striving to influence and transform our work people, places and policies, so that they might reflect the values of the Kingdom of God.

The role of the corps is to equip its soldiers for this challenge. We have already mentioned the importance of focusing our ministry within a particular geographical area. Yet in most Western nations this isolated view will need to develop and expand significantly. The reality is many of our best people now need to have a dual focus. Often people who live in cities, do not work in the same area and community where they live or worship, hence their mission at work and their mission within the local corps community, need to be seen as two very distinct areas of mission. (For those who work, live and worship in three separate communities, theirs is the constant challenge of connecting with their own community. If recent history has taught us anything, it is the impotence of 'commuting' corps to reach their communities geographically.)

Sadly the Church has not been very good at this and has perpetuated a dualistic view of vocation separating their secular and sacred ministries, leaving many unsupported and disempowered for their ministry in the workplace. I have a friend who works at a very senior level in the world of leadership training and development, connecting with some of the most influential multi-national corporations in the world. She expressed her frustration with this unhelpful dualism by stating, 'my ministry is amongst the movers and shakers of the leadership world yet all my church is concerned about is whether or not I will take a Sunday school class.' This is not to decry the importance of local church ministry but rather to recognise the essential dual focus of many of our people. If we are to encourage our people to own their mission for the market place or for the home makers their local community, they need to be envisioned and resourced appropriately.

We need to be envisioning the emerging generations to view themselves as entering their chosen career, in whatever field they choose, as an instrument of change. Every Christian is a 'full-time Christian worker', the only distinction being their sphere of influence. As Keith Green the musician used to say, there are two types of people in the world – 'mission-field' (unsaved) or 'missionaries' (saved). We need millions of men and women and boys and girls who will see themselves as called and gifted to take the good news of the gospel out into the market place to reach our lost world on the front-line of life. I believe the future effectiveness of The Salvation Army is largely dependent upon its ability to envision and mobilise its members in terms of living out this 'whole-life' mission.

The Secular Franciscan Order exists to facilitate this kind of commitment within the Roman Catholic tradition. It resources Roman Catholic Christians to live out the Franciscan ideals in their work-day environments, thus enabling people to move from Gospel to life and from life to Gospel. This salt and light ministry has sought to carry the Gospel and the ideals of this movement into every sphere of society. Envisioning its members to bring the transformational and redemptive power of the Gospel to bear upon their workplace, environment and cultures.

For many of our people, whenever the 'call' is mentioned it signals a switching on of the guilt and frustration buttons. Guilt, because they have not sensed any 'call' in the direction of officership vocation which has too often been the only one recognised and affirmed. Frustration, because they have then carried that guilt and subsequent lack of affirmation into the arena of their workplace and genuine 'call'. I believe this has had a devastating impact upon the effectiveness of our mission within the world and as well as recruitment into the role of officership.

Big C and Little c

I have often found it very helpful to talk of 'calling' in terms of a big C (calling) and a little c. The big C represents God's big picture call upon your life; that is the realm where you will seek to exert your primary influence. For some of my friends this is the world of education, others the world of medicine or finance, still for others, local community. For me my big C is The Salvation Army. This is the area where I am called to exert the maximum amount of influence in seeing this movement best fulfil its God-given mandate.

The little c represents the specific details within the bigger picture. I am unsure as to what my particular role within The Salvation Army will be. That I need to trust and seek God for, but I have clarified the bigger picture question and so can be very focused in what I do. Many of us spend much of our time trying to work out the secondary question without knowing the first. It may be helpful for those unclear as to their 'call' to identify initially the **realm** of their calling, before worrying about the **role**.

The leadership and management gurus of our day state that we get the best out of people by enabling them to do and be what they most naturally are. Our greatest strengths are found in doing those things that we can't help but do and these are often most powerfully demonstrated when our vocation is matched by these natural skills and giftings. The world that we are called to win for God is in reality made up of different worlds. Consequently we need warriors fighting at every level and in every sphere of that world. Battles need to be fought in the world of education, commerce, politics, medicine, the media and the arts. Those who have an interest in particular to areas like the media and the arts, I want to encourage in every way to seek their way within those arenas. The level of the influence these specific areas have is quite incredible and again it is a world that needs to be won.

So much of the future effectiveness of The Salvation Army will largely be determined by our ability to empower and envision people to reach their worlds. The influence of salvationism, its vision, values and passion must be brought to bear within the diverse realms of our rapidly-changing world. The front-line soldiers must recognise this essential nature of their role and begin to view their vocation not merely as a means for financial reward but rather as the field of battle upon which they fight.

The How

How on earth are we to win these battles for the will? Trusting in the power of the Holy Spirit is an essential dynamic in the process, but one perspective that is often missed is that of strong and healthy accountable relationships. Western individualism has robbed many cultures of any sense of community. Tragically, as so often has occurred, the Church has baptised this culture of isolation, and privatised many aspects of life and discipleship that should come within the realm of communal consideration and accountability.

Whether it be the issue of budgetary control, relational decisions or just the general issues of living out faith, we all need some safe people and places to assist us in steering the right course.

Scripture is quite explicit on these issues in encouraging us towards having adequate support networks in place. As we shall see, the relationships between Paul and Timothy, Elijah and Elisha, David and Jonathan; Jesus, Peter, James and John all reflect these types of friendships. It goes well beyond the 'spilling coffee' fellowship at the church on Sunday. These are relationships of depth and intimacy; risk and vulnerability are at their heart.

- **Ecclesiastes 4:9–12** – This whole passage makes it clear that the strength of team and relational commitment is essential for effective work and protection during the battle. Picking up when fallen down (v. 10), defending when attacked (v. 12), and finishing with the famous line: *'A cord of three strands is not quickly broken.'*

- **Proverbs 27:17** – *'As iron sharpens iron, so one man sharpens another.'* Mutual accountability brings an edge and honing to our lives as we serve together. Looking for the best in each other, observing development and holding to account on agreed ideals is essential for the maturing of a warrior.
- **1 Samuel 20:17, 42** – We see here a solemn covenant of friendship, love, commitment and accountability. Their relationship was focused on seeking the best for one another and calling each other on in their service for God.

In terms of New Testament models we need look no further than the ministry of Jesus himself. He called the Twelve 'to be with him,' I believe, not only for their benefit and preparation but for his own support and encouragement. As fully God and fully man he needed people in the same way that all humans need people. I believe his three closest friends, Peter, James and John were his support group. As we can see from his asking for their support at the Garden of Gethsemane, he needed their moral, relational and physical support at the point where he was most likely to compromise his call and role in the war (Matthew 26:36–46).

Allowing the above to be an accurate assessment of the role of the disciples, it faces us with the powerful challenge that if the incarnate Son of God needed people to make it and remain consistent, then **how much more do we need it?** The imposed privatisation of Western individualism is not only unbiblical but practically disastrous, leaving many warriors isolated and vulnerable in their fight. We all need safe, accountable relationships if the battle for the heart is to be won.

Accountability – More Lone Rangers Needed?

Often the term 'lone ranger' has been used to describe an isolated Christian or Christian leader just doing their own thing outside of any real relationships of substance or community. This I have always found confusing as 'The Lone Ranger', an old TV character was not truly alone; he always had his sidekick Tonto with him. What we need is a lot more lone rangers in that kind of deep committed friendship.

Contemporary Christian history is littered with examples of high-profile Christian leaders who, for lack of viable accountability, have made decisions that have ended their own ministry, damaged the lives of many others and brought the gospel into disrepute. For those who would be warriors, accountability is a non-negotiable absolute. Much misunderstanding has abounded about this subject and so it is important to define our terms before moving on. In truth, accountability can only ever be given, it cannot be imposed. We are called to account for those things that we have asked to be challenged about or are contracted to fulfil. I can only be held to account for those things that I ask for, or have previously agreed to. It is not about control or dominance but rather commitment in seeking the best for another, calling them on and supporting them in striving after God's best.

Three models

In the years that I have been involved with and taught on this subject, I have found three models of these relationships that are most easily adopted in many diverse situations.

Support group – This closely follows the model of Jesus. He was part of a small group of people who held common visions and committed themselves to hold each other to account to the agreed ideals. The group would probably meet weekly for prayer, encouragement and perhaps Bible study. I have known of groups that committed themselves to ask each other specific questions about lifestyle, business practice, family life etc. everytime they met, setting goals for development and advancement in specific areas of life.

They will cover one another in prayer at particular times, give advice and counsel when required and help each other to discern and live out the will of God for their lives. So often I meet people struggling in isolation to 'discover their call' when it is most likely to be found amongst a group of people who know you well, believe in you and are committed to you. Sometimes warriors get a Macedonian call, as in the case of Paul in Acts 16:6–10 when he got a very specific visional revelation from God. But in my experience it is the exception rather than the rule.

Peer support – This is akin to the deep friendship that Jesus appeared to have with the apostle John or the covenant friendship that David and Jonathan shared. I have such a relationship with Ian Mayhew (leader of my corps). We have been seeking to support one another for about nine years and the depth and parameters of the friendship has developed over that time. We have moved from an occasional phone call and meal together to what is now a weekly early breakfast to connect with one another in a number of different ways.

We meet to encourage one another, listen and respond to the issues we are wrestling with, pray and study God's word together. I have asked Ian to call me to account for the ideals I have regarding who I am as a husband, father, leader, evangelist etc. He can ask me any question that he likes and in the covenant of our friendship I am committed to speaking the truth. When I am discouraged he supports me, when I am confused he helps bring clarity and understanding, When I have been out of order, he has rebuked me. When I want to give up, he calls me on and drags me out my despair. (NB. My wife is totally at ease with the friendship and our parameters of dialogue are largely established by what she is comfortable with. For those of us who are married, this is very important.)

The support has included letters of encouragement at key times, occasional retreats, travelling and ministry together, buying and sharing books that have challenged each other. Without stressing it too highly I believe that this support has been one of the key factors in my still being in the role of leadership that I at present fulfil. This kind of support takes time to develop but it is well worth the effort and is very strategic for active warriors. I believe it is vitally important for those in leadership.

I have a little equation that I think is essential for leaders to consider:

$$L–T–A = L$$

Put in full it reads:

Leaders – Team – Accountability = Liability

I have met so many hurting and vulnerable leaders who for want of this support wrestle with crushing loneliness and insecurity. I have wept and prayed with leaders who have compromised the call of God upon their life because there was no 'friend' they trusted in place to call them to account. As Jesus needed a team (Matthew 26:38), as Timothy needed to be accountable to Paul (2 Timothy 1:6) as David needed the protection of Jonathan (1 Samuel 20:13), so we too need that kind of support. Pray for God to provide those support networks and seek the protection and encouragement that only they can provide.

In working in a close-knit team/community environment it is difficult to compromise your ideals, as those around you can bear witness to the integrity or otherwise of your life. One of the reasons I rarely travel alone is because of my temptation to exaggerate stories etc. when preaching. This is untenable when someone sitting in front of you works or worships with you and knows the truth. Hypocrisy can only hide for so long in close proximity to those who know you best.

Couples – Obviously, a married couple are very much a team in terms of their ministry. I find accountability with another couple helpful and supportive. My wife and I regularly meet with other married couples to share struggles over children, family life and even budgets. We have just begun to share with one couple our budgetary goals for the year and desire a degree of accountability within the security of this friendship and the wider accountability of community. This provides some of the broader support network that God intended within the extended family and community.

Martin Luther had stood alone in the ecclesiastical court and by the grace of God managed to win that battle for his will, yet this isolation is not the ideal, nor God's design.

Some of the above may seem quite extreme or even bizarre to readers considering these issues for the first time, yet I believe them to be sound biblical principles which if applied wisely with good accountability, can help prepare and protect in the war. We were not designed to fight alone, we always need someone to watch our back. We all need others who will stand and fight for our will.

Chapter 5

Victories Future

What kind of warrior will you be?

In 1993, I was driving on the M40, on my way to preach at a small Salvation Army corps. The topic that I had been asked to speak on was 'The Urgency of Vision.' It was a warm evening and I kept glancing over at the sun on my right. It was one of those perfect sunsets which spread an orange glow over everything. I was feeling completely relaxed and mentally rehearsed what I was going to say that evening. Vision is a subject I have always enjoyed talking about and I remember planning my opening. I was going to tell a joke about an optician, and then make the statement:

> *'Vision is not only about being able to see – it is about where we choose to look.'*

'Vision,' I would then say, 'is all about urgency.'

The urgency of the gospel, cruising steadily at 70 mph, thinking of how I would preach, was about to come clearly into view. I heard, rather than saw, the car crash up ahead of me. As soon as the sound was heard the road ahead was lit up with the accumulative glow of scores of brake lights. The pile-up, involving numerous cars was significant. I had arrived just moments after the initial accident had taken place; the police and ambulance services were not yet on the scene. There were cars strewn all over the road, some facing the opposite direction, some on their roofs, some had slid down the roadside bank, others were a mass of tangled metal and plastic. The smell of burning rubber and oil filled the air, smoke and dust still clouding the skies.

I got out and tried to give help where I could. I came across one car that had a family in it. The husband was dead in the central reservation. The mother and older child were trapped in the back, crushed down underneath the flattened roof, yet still alive. I saw pieces of a baby carrier, its shattered fragments all around the car. Then I came across the baby, some yards from the vehicle, 2–3 months old, lying dead in the middle of the fast lane. Many people were trying to help those in need, others just stood too distressed to move or act.

By now the emergency services had arrived in force. A policeman covered the little one with his coat, firemen began to try and cut the woman and child out of the back of the car. I began trying to stop members of the public who had stopped to look from getting in the way. A group of football supporters returning home in a hired coach had got out to see what was causing the traffic jam. They moved en masse towards the carnage, and stood stunned by the scene that lay before them. Just as I went to try to usher them back, they began tying their football scarves around the road barrier as a mark of respect; most left in tears, devastated by what they had seen.

Later I came across the police photographer. He had taken many pictures of some awful things in his time but never a baby dead in the road. He was obviously struggling with this and allowed me to pray for him. 'This is the first baby,' he kept saying under his breath, struggling to come to terms with what he had seen. With so many of the emergency services on the scene, having spoken with a few of the younger policemen, I left to continue my journey.

All of this consumed my mind for days. The lights, the tears, the scarves. The fragility of life. The precious infant in the road. I don't believe that I spoke particularly well later on that evening. I was in no fit state to educate anyone about the 'Urgency of Vision.' Yet more than at any other time in my life, I began to **understand** it.

The reason that we must win the battles for our heart, our mind and our will is that there is a desperate need for people who are **free** to obey God. Once we have won them, it is vital that we direct our lives according to God's vision, not our own.

Victims of Vision

In the Western world, vision was one of the casualties of the 1980s. A generation was sold the lie that to have is to be happy, and that the only thing worth living for was your piece of the corporate pie. This myth failed to deliver the goods and has left people passionless and resigned to an inevitable second-best that breeds an insidious and crippling hopelessness. In both the socio-political and spiritual realm, the status quo has reigned supreme for too long. If we are to fight effectively, this must be dethroned in our lives and corps.

Only vision has the power to break this cycle of negativity. It paints a picture of a preferable future across the canvas of people's minds and injects hope into hearts of despair. Every revolution has begun with a vision, an image of what could be, a dream of something so vividly seen but as yet unrealised. I believe every warrior must identify their individual and corporate vision that will be the driving force of their lives. That thing that will get them up in the morning, keep them working into the night and at times keep them awake during the night. It is the kindling of potential that has changed nations. The vision of The World for God ignited the hearts of early Salvationists, who gave themselves unreservedly to its dynamism. It is only the presence of a lofty vision that can save the ailing religious systems of many a denomination and bring intentional focus to the lives of those within it.

I meet so many Christians who find themselves idling in neutral for the want of vision. Certainly committed, but living confused and defused lives, their energies dissipated, minimising their impact within the world. It is the romance and passion of vision that warms the true warrior in the cold nights of despair and frustration. It is vision that forces them to dig to the very depths of who they are in God, as they pay the price of what it means to be a victim of vision.

Vision is not primarily about what I do but rather who I am. My personal vision is to help bring back to The Salvation Army some of those things that have been lost. I believe passionately that The Salvation Army is potentially one of the most effective tools for fulfilling the Great Commission. The excluded of the world included. We could see hundreds of thousands of lives transformed by the gospel, but I believe this is only viable with a return to the militancy and radical commitment of our roots. Hence no matter what I do in life I will be seeking to see this vision realised. As a husband, father, leader, evangelist or friend, I will be pursuing this dream. Irrespective of my circumstances, this is the focus of my energies and that to which I seek to give myself to. It is primarily an issue of 'being' rather than 'doing.'

Capturing That Vision

In seeking God for my vision, I 'breathe in' my **being**, then 'breathe out' my **doing**. My actions are determined by what I am committed to, as the fruit of my vision. Everything I am, I express, I value, I produce, becomes a vehicle for crying out the vision that God has given me. The big question for many of us is how we get that vision for which we might live.

In Genesis, God speaks to Abraham at a strategic point in his life, just after Lot has left him (Genesis 13:14). I am sure this was a time of change and insecurity for Abraham, as he set out on his own and faced new challenges. These are often the times when God can speak to us most clearly, when the securities of our lives are shifting and changing, giving opportunity for new direction and fresh ideas. Too regularly, we view these times negatively when in reality they are threshold times when new things can come into being or vision can come into much greater clarity.

Vision Begins Where You Are

In the midst of this time God says to Abraham:

> *'Lift up your eyes from where you are and look north and south, east and west.'* (Genesis 13:14)

Vision began 'from where he was' as it does for us. It begins with an honest assessment of who and where we are. Vision has been defined as:

> 'Dreams plus reality.'

In finding our vision the following are some of the realities needing to be understood and appreciated if we are to map a way to live out the vision that God brings to us. It maybe good to discuss these with a close friend or write them down in a spiritual journal or even a write a letter to God to get an appropriate appreciation of where you are.

- Knowing who we are – our skills, our spiritual gifts personality, passions, dreams, experience all add up to who we are.
- Knowing God, his will and work in our life thus far, the lessons he has taught us, issues he has laid on our hearts, his character, his word, the input and advice of his people.
- Knowing the situation you are in – the circumstances of those around you, the world you live in, your corps/church, your society.

All these things add up to a recognition of where we are, which is essential in discovering our vision. Too often I meet people chasing a vision whose lives are in a terrible mess. Inconsistency is their motto. They have never stuck at anything, they consistently make choices which inhibit growth and effectiveness. These are not disqualifications for being used by God but until they are dealt with, they will consistently limit your usefulness. You may be in the wrong relationship or the wrong job and these things need recognising as the starting point for vision.

Vision Determines What You See

God didn't end it there with Abraham but encouraged him not only to 'lift' his eyes above his present circumstances but to look and see what he could see.

> *'All the land that you see I will give to you and your offspring for ever.'* (Genesis 13:15)

God's vision for our lives is not limited to the present situation but encourages us to lift our viewing above that context to see new possibilities. Vision by definition is seeing the invisible, the unattained, that which is not yet achieved or seemingly possible. It is that which with foresight seems impossible but with hindsight appeared inevitable.

I have found that one of the most important ingredients in vision is our belief in what we believe God is capable of. Imagine the childless nomad Abraham just being told that he would birth a nation that would inhabit a land of their own, yet we are told he 'believed God' and so God fulfilled his promise. I sometimes catch myself thinking like an atheist in various situations whereby the only consideration in my thinking is that which already exists. So often God's capacity to fulfil visions and dreams is limited by our capacity to 'believe God' and receive.

An essential aspect of gaining a vision is that God is *'able to do more than we can imagine or even think of'* (Ephesians 3:20). Your start does not have to be your story; God is a God of new beginnings and as you seek after his vision for your life, it is essential to 'believe God.' He is not limited to the present circumstances. Recently I have been struggling with real doubts about the most significant and largest programme our team runs. Self-doubt, fear, insecurity all came my way and then I was reminded one day, whilst reading my devotional book in the bath, of the passage in Romans recounting Abraham's response to God's vision.

> *'Yet he did not waver through unbelief regarding the promise of God, but was strengthened in his faith and gave glory to God, being **fully persuaded** that God had the power to do what he had promised.'* (Romans 4:20–21)

Vision is grasped by those who are 'fully persuaded.' This being so, go about looking to discover that vision. Taking all the information you have assessed at the beginning, start down the most obvious path, walk through the most obvious door and trust God to make it right. God is not a teaser who will keep us guessing but desires more than us that we grasp our vision. He will soon make it clear if we have gone in the wrong direction. I have heard it said that 'the need is the call,' I personally don't agree, but a good place to start is by seeking to meet the most obvious needs you can. It is as we actively seek and work that God can do most with us. It is very difficult to steer a stationary vehicle anywhere, it must be going somewhere.

Finally, my experience has led me to believe that few of us get a Macedonian vision like the apostle Paul but most of us work out our vision in line with those whose dreams we share, and with those we want to be in relationship with, whether people or an institution. Again, my total vision is wrapped up with The Salvation Army and so any question regarding my focus comes within that framework. A friend of mine is a senior financial executive, and knows that God wants him to seek to influence and shape within that environment; so again the framework is set. Other friends are part of corps and churches because they sense a call to work with particular people whose vision they share. This is how our Movement began; with people sharing common vision and values. Its future will be largely determined by decisions of a similar type.

Vision Decides What You Do

Having established something of a vision the next step for Abraham was to actually 'do something' about it.

> *'Go, walk through the length and breadth of the land, for I am giving it to you.'*   (Genesis 13:17)

This vision was not to be some kind of ethereal concept that hung around in the space between Abraham's ears, but rather a whole new direction for life and focus for his future that had to be acted upon. There is a form of 'spirituality' that is common in the Church, which says that all we need to do is 'let go and let God;' all we need to do is pray and the Lord will sort it out. This sounds so spiritual and pious, but in real terms is biblical nonsense. To sit back and do nothing whilst expecting God to do everything is not faith but superstition.

As Abraham began to get hold of the vision, he had to practise the vision. This is essential to grounding early tenets of vision within us. Following are four very simple ways of doing this.

Write it – Script out your vision, draw it, memorise it, stick a copy of it on your wall or fridge. Articulating your vision in a way that has shape and clarity is very helpful. We are told by the management gurus that an important step in seeing change take place within a major institution is for every employee to be able to articulate the company's vision in one or two sentences. It helps the philosophy of the vision to get fully soaked up into our consciousness and automatically becomes a sieve through which all future possibilities must pass.

Pray it – This sounds quite obvious but again is essential to our vision becoming the all-consuming passion it needs be. Creativity may be helpful at this point. For about 18 months I wore a small leather bracelet as a constant reminder to pray for a particular aspect of my vision. At present I carry a small credit-card-sized card that has three questions on to focus my prayer around an aspect of my vision. Prayer will build the intensity of focus needed as well as calling down the power and blessing of God upon it.

Share it – Vision needs to be shared to enable others to own its agenda as well as having others to call you to account for it. Individual dreams have little chance of having any impact unless others own and commit to it, so sharing the vision in an accessible form is of strategic importance.

Be wise with whom you share it, don't surround yourself with 'Yes' people who will agree with anything and everything irrespective of the consequences. This said, you must also avoid the 'vision killers.' I find they exist in most religious institutions. They have an almost prophetic ability to think of ten reasons why something can't happen. Find fellow 'dreamers' who will journey with you discovering all the creative possibilities for your vision.

Do it – Set yourself some goals, take some action that will begin to take you towards the fulfilment of the vision. This needs to be thought through in terms of its timescale and how it will affect your current lifestyle and commitments. Begin with the ideal, don't accept second-best as your starting point. I have often been called naive because I am an idealist, but idealism isn't the opposite of realism. Beginning with a high ideal always lifts our expectation and creates a hunger after excellence. Aim high, and you may not reach everything but you will still achieve much more than accepting second-best as your starting point. I tend to find much cynicism and negativity hidden under the cloak of so-called 'realism.'

The reckless abandon of early Salvationists made them 'eyeballers of the future'. Those who saw themselves not as victims of that future but rather shapers of the future. That was the power of their vision. A vision that isn't acted upon is a barrel of possibility that could have been but never was, assigned to the dregs of disappointment, stirred regularly with the spoon of regret.

Vision Defines Who You Are

Finally Abraham had to obey and move. God had given him the vision, he knew what it was God wanted him to do, yet he still had to obey.

> *'So Abram moved his tents and went to live near the great trees of Mamre at Hebron, where he built an altar to the Lord.'*
> (Genesis 13:18)

The vision was not to be fulfilled for hundreds of years, yet Abraham had to begin to live in the light of the vision irrespective of the circumstances. Living in the light of that which as yet does not exist is the essence of vision and integral to seeing it become a reality.

Pastor Paul Yonggi Cho, pastor of the largest church in the world in Seoul, Korea, tells of the day that God told him he was to have a church of three thousand people. At the time he led a church of fifteen people, most of whom were his family who met in an old US Army tent. Yet he began to preach as though there were three thousand in the tent. When his congregation asked him to quieten down and stop shouting, he retorted that God had told him to act, live and preach as though he had already seen the vision realised, so this he did. Many years later he has a church of 750,000, including 15 deaf people!

Vision is not something we wait around for hoping to happen but rather something that we precipitate by our actions. We hasten its arrival, we ache and long for its consummation, yet it never arrives. Vision by definition never fully arrives; it is always out there, calling us on. Frustration at its failure to be fully realised is not an enemy to be resisted but rather a friend to be embraced. 'Frustration is a friend of mine' should be one of our buzz phrases as it is a constant reminder that we are still in vision and have not settled down. Show me a fully satisfied man or woman and I will show you someone who has lost their vision.

Dealers in Hope

This process of living in the light of that which is yet to be, is called 'hope.' Warriors need to be people of hope. Tielhard de Chardin stated that the future belongs to those who can give it hope and he is right. A world that has lost its vision of a brighter, better future and has surrendered to the stranglehold of hopelessness, desperately needs people who will live a life and dream a vision of hope. Scripture has never been more true than when declaring, *'Where there is no vision, people perish.'*

The following prose demonstrates this well.

> Lost in the world of darkness, without a guiding light
> Seeking a friend to help my struggling failing plight.
> Now all of you good people just go on passing by,
> Leaving me with nothing but this likely will to die.
>
> Somewhere in this lonely world of sorrow and of woe
> there's a place for me to hide, but where I do not
>   know;
> For no matter where I go I never will escape
> the devil's reaching, clutching hands,
> or the drink of fermented grape.
>
> So out of my grief and anguish, perhaps some
>   wandering boy will see,
> Long after I have left this world
> And build his own life, strong and good and free.

The tragedy of this is not only its close proximity to the ambience and zeitgeist of the emerging generations, but that it was not written as a poetical reflection of society: but it was the suicide note of a fifteen-year-old American boy.

Napoleon Bonaparte believed that leaders (warriors) needed to be 'dealers in hope.' Those who, no matter what the circumstances, would hold on to the dream and never let go. These 'dealers' need to constantly infect others with the virus of hope, lifting their vision beyond the morass of difficulty and opposition. The early days are often the most exciting but very quickly the challenges of the vision come to the fore and at this point we need to dig very deep and keep focused on the task in hand. Most of us want to live on the mountain top to where our vision calls us, but the reality is that visions take shape in the hard graft of the valley. We celebrate on the mountain top, we bring it to birth in the valley.

Dealers in hope are those that infect others with their vision. Within a part of American Indian culture enormous respect was given to the water carriers, those that brought fresh water into the village each day. Far from being considered menial, they were essential as they brought the water of life to the people. We need to be water carriers or, in our terms, vision carriers. We bring life to those around us; every time we bump into people we 'splash' them with our vision. Those with whom we spend longer we soak with it; we are constantly bringing life to the community we are part of and to those that we meet. I have a friend who is a real water carrier. I think every time I have heard him speak he has expanded my own vision, even fanned into flame something new. When I speak with him one-to-one I am challenged about my own lack of vision and called on to new depths of commitment to it. He is truly a dealer in hope. People like him are the answer to Paul's prayer to the Romans:

> *'May the God of hope fill you with all joy and peace as you trust in him, so that you may **overflow** with hope by the power of the Holy Spirit.'* (Romans 15:13)

Revisit your vision regularly, like Abraham who built an altar; have those places and times of remembrance, particularly when times get hard. Vision has power. Power to unite, as Jim Wallis states:

> '...the only route to common ground is to take people to higher ground.'

Power to sacrifice, inspire and motivate. Vision is the seed of revolution.

Wallis tells the story of eating a meal with a black family in a Soweto township during the late 1980s. There was still a lot of violence around and particularly stiff retribution for those demanding and demonstrating for change. There was a particularly precocious fifteen-year-old at the table. Wallis engaged him in conversation and asked him if he thought his grandchildren would ever breathe the air of freedom in South Africa. At this point the young man went silent. Staring at the table he stood up, pushed his shoulders back, stared Wallis in the face and said, 'I will see to it that they do.' That's vision.

True warriors provide the much needed prophetic mantle as they lift up vision, flying counter to the pervading negativity of the day. Their lives call others on to the biblical images of Isaiah 65 and Revelation 21, herald of a new way of being, marching to the rhythm of another drum.

> ' "Behold, I will create new heavens and a new earth. The former things will not be remembered, nor will they come to mind. But be glad and rejoice for ever in what I will create, for I will create Jerusalem to be a delight and its people a joy ... the sound of weeping and of crying will be heard in it no more. Never again will there be in it an infant who lives but a few days, or an old man who does not live out his years ... They will build houses and dwell in them; they will plant vineyards and eat their fruit ... They will not toil in vain or bear children doomed to misfortune; for they will be a people blessed by the Lord ... The wolf and the lamb will feed together, and the lion will eat straw like the ox ... They will neither harm nor destroy on all my holy mountain," says the Lord.'* (Isaiah 65:17–25)

> 'Then I saw a new heaven and a new earth, for the first heaven and the first earth had passed away, and there was no longer any sea. I saw the Holy City, the new Jerusalem, coming down out of heaven from God, prepared as a bride*

beautifully dressed for her husband. And I heard a loud voice from the throne saying, "Now the dwelling of God is with men, and he will live with them. They will be his people, and God himself will be with them and be their God. He will wipe every tear from their eyes. There will be no more death or mourning or crying or pain, for the old order of things has passed away." '

(Revelation 21:1–4)

These are the biblical images of a new reality, a vision of hope, a picture of things to come. Paradise regained, justice done, the peace and wholeness of God lived in perfection throughout the created order. It is this future reality that must always be held out in front of us, it must inform and shape all our dreams and plans. No matter how hard things get or how dire they appear, this is our guaranteed future, ultimate reality. We must strive for this in our present, knowing it is only a foretaste of what will be.

Vision carriers are those who live in the constant paradox of remembrance and anticipation. Constantly encouraged by remembering what God has already done and living in expectancy and anticipation of all he says he is going to do. They are tomorrow people, living today in the light of what will be.

Warriors need to be so encapsulated by the vision of the gospel that they will live for it and if necessary die for it. As Martin Luther King is so well known for reciting:

'A man who won't die for something is not fit to live.' [53]

The cost is counted, the dream consumed, the vision lifted up now we must, like our young South African brother, just 'See to it!'

The Way of the Cross

There are many things in the Bible that are at times difficult to understand and others open to a number of differing interpretations. Yet on the issue of the basics of what it means to follow Jesus no such confusion exists. Jesus makes it very clear:

> *'If anyone would come after me, he must deny himself and take up his cross and follow me.'*   (Mark 8:34)

Jesus made it very clear to all who would consider becoming part of his Kingdom that a great deal of cost would be involved in living out the consequences of that decision. The apostle Paul understood this all too well when he wrote to the Corinthian church reminding them of the lengths to which he had been willing to go to achieve the Kingdom goals (2 Corinthians 11:23–29). He went on to remind Timothy that anyone seeking to live a Jesus-type life would inevitably face scorn and persecution from the world around him (2 Timothy 3:12). Before being called Christians, early believers were known as people of 'the Way' and this was consistently the way of the cross. For those of us who would seek to live a life and fight a battle that counts, the same will be true. To journey along the road of the Jesus-way is to set a collision course with hardship and difficulty.

This kind of teaching does not sit well within so many of our comfort-driven cultures, which have lifted up another god to be worshipped, creating the idolatry of comfort. Pain must be avoided at all costs so that this new object of our worship might be satisfied. It is what I call the 'softening of the saints.' Rather than battle-hardened warriors we have become cushion-padded ponderers, reflecting on the niceties of our religious systems and customs, whilst the battle rages outside our doors. We have even shaped our theologies to sanctify our comfort orientation. There are the conservatives who wallow in nostalgia, turning memories of victories past into the cause of defeats present and future. The charismatics who have invented the health and wealth heresy that influenced many by creating a

Church which resists all prices to be paid by labelling it the 'work of the enemy.'

The theology of the Spirit has been perverted more at this point than any other. Somehow we have come to believe that the Spirit is given to bless us, anoint us, empower us for our own benefit. Yet Scripture is clear, as believed by our forebears, that the Spirit blesses so that we might bless others. He ministers to us so that we might minister to others. It is amazing how many times I have heard preachers talking about the 'Pentecostal experience' of the book of Acts and inviting people to come forward and receive it. Yet do they realise what they are saying? After the coming of the Spirit had caused a physical shaking of the house, the immediate fruit was sacrificial costly living in the lives of those who received. I have never heard an appeal asking people to come forward for empowerment so that they might have the power to cope with the pain of obedient sacrifice. Yet this is part of the package of the warrior life – the power to cope with the pain.

Tragically this comfort orientation has heralded the demise of many would-be warriors who turn away at the point of cost, choosing the way of least resistance and subsequently missing the opportunity for victory and advance. The old maxim 'No pain – No gain' from the sporting world holds so true for the Christian life, as often our greatest steps forward only come at the point of greatest pain. Anyone who has pushed their physical body hard in the pursuit of excellence, will know that it is the last few repetitions, the last few yards that bring the greatest pain yet the most benefit as the pain barrier is crossed and defeated. A lifestyle that seeks to avoid the knocks and damage of the battle lays hold of what Bonhoeffer called 'cheap grace', receiving the free love-offering of God's grace, then refusing to live out the consequence of receiving such gift.

There is not such a thing as a 'painless war'. Infra-red guidance systems used in the Gulf War may have given us the idea that such a thing can exist but it is a myth;

someone always pays the price. This Army needs warriors who will stare in the face of opposition and hardship and push on regardless, recognising any scars picked up on the way as battle medals to be worn with appropriate pride. William Booth was once spat upon and when a friend moved to wipe the spittle from his beard Booth held him back saying, 'Leave them alone, they are battle scars.' It needs to be the expectation of serious warriors that significant cost will be involved.

We have also perverted our theology of what it means to be a Christian conqueror. They are not those who have avoided all cost and pain but rather those who have kept going and persevered through it. The apostle Paul defines this for us well:

> *'We put no stumbling-block in anyone's path, so that our ministry will not be discredited. Rather, as servants of God we commend ourselves in every way: in great endurance; in troubles, hardships and distresses; in beatings, imprisonments and riots; in hard work, sleepless nights and hunger; in purity, understanding, patience and kindness; in the Holy Spirit and in sincere love; in truthful speech and in the power of God; with weapons of righteousness in the right hand and in the left; through glory and dishonour, bad report and good report; genuine, yet regarded as impostors; known, yet regarded as unknown; dying, and yet we live on; beaten and yet not killed; sorrowful, yet always rejoicing; poor, yet making many rich; having nothing, and yet possessing everything.'*
>
> (2 Corinthians 6:3–10)

The way of the cross is the way of the warrior. There is no other way. The following song expresses well the true nature of Christian conquerors.

Conquerors

Tomorrow is a brand new day
and all my sins have been washed away.

My hands look new
My life free
My heart is pure
I have been redeemed

I've seen His face
I've touched His hands
Finally, now I understand
Why He died for a wretch like me
And by His blood
I have been redeemed

We ran the race
We kept the fight
We shed our blood
For what was right
We carried our cross
Through storm and rain
Because of Christ
Now we can say
We are conquerors

So no matter what we're going through
We are conquerors
I'm going to give all my life to you
We are conquerors

Gethsemane Moment

For many of us our sharing in the sufferings of Christ is something we naturally want to shy away from. Who wants pain, hardship and difficulty? But face it we must, and also realise that most of our suffering as a Christian comes as a result of a choice we must make firstly to face, and then embrace, our suffering. Occasionally hardship is directly imposed upon us but mostly it comes when we choose to stand up and make our faith count in the war of salvation in our world.

The numerous stories of the experiences of Jesus in the

Garden of Gethsemane are a challenging model for facing our own Gethsemane moment. I often say that I believe that our salvation was sealed in the Garden, for up until that point Jesus' destiny was very much in his own hands, after that point it was very much in the hands of others. He had a choice, he could have backed away but he chose to walk the way of the cross. Having walked into the Garden, he knelt by the stone to consider his options and face his suffering. Matthew's version is particularly stirring:

> *'My Father, if it is not possible for this cup to be taken away unless I drink it, may your will be done.'*
>
> (Matthew 26:42)

He faced his suffering, counted the cost and realised it was only in his embracing this suffering by walking out of the Garden to face his betrayer, that God's divine will would be done.

I have had the privilege of spending some time with Christians who had suffered significantly for their faith. It was in Ethiopia which at that time was still under the communist dictator Mengistu. I met them at a secret Bible study in the house of a man who had just come out of prison having served a seven-year sentence for being an elder of a church. As I sat in this meeting, filled with men who had all been in prison at some time for their faith, the presence of God was quite overpowering. I remember weeping during the worship, having been faced with the question in meeting these brothers of how far I was willing to go.

This is a fundamental question that each warrior must face. The cost must be counted; how far will you go? My good friends, to whom I have dedicated this book, are Captains Geoff and Sandra Ryan. They are imperfect people, ask anyone who knows them, but they have asked this question and have had to live with the consequences of their answer.

They opened the work of The Salvation Army in Russia in

the city of St. Petersburg. When going to the country they covenanted to each other that they would seek to live as those they were going to serve in terms of lifestyle, economics, health care etc. Sandra had a miscarriage and when she became pregnant for a second time she became incredibly ill, in part due to the unsanitary conditions of the hospital and the limited care facilities. The Salvation Army has an insurance policy on them that provides for private care in Finland but because of their covenant to live like those they were serving, Sandra remained in the Russian hospital. A point came whereby Sandra was critically ill and so Geoff was in the position of having to make the decisions on his own about what to do. If he now moved her from the hospital the child would die and he would break the covenant principle they had made. If he left her where she was both Sandra and the baby could die.

I telephoned him during this time and he shared with me the pressure he was under from various quarters to take Sandra to Finland. We discussed the issues knowing that we were talking about people's lives, during which Geoff said, regarding the covenant that they had made, 'Everybody is telling me to get her out of the country, but a principle is not a principle until you have to put it into practice: up until then it's just a good idea.' Everything within me wanted to tell him to take Sandra to Finland but I agreed that night to stand with him in the decision that he had made to leave her in the Russian hospital as per their covenant, and face whatever consequences that might bring.

The story continues with the child being miscarried and Sandra eventually, after a long recuperation, recovering. They now have an adopted son as well as a very healthy twelve-month-old son of their own. Because of the decisions they made to seek to live like those they were called to serve, Sandra will be a hepatitis B carrier for the rest of her life.

I am sure there are those reading this who would disagree vehemently with the decision that they made and in talking with them I know that, looking back, they are also unsure in their own clarity on the issue. The point of including the story isn't to say what is right or wrong, but rather to highlight the issue that they and every warrior must face. To engage in a war is to make a decision to embrace suffering. The question they have encountered and which I and maybe others reading this book have still to face is, how far am I willing to go? The issues will no doubt be different for us all whether it be our relationships, our possessions, our popularity or our career. The question for each of us warriors is – will we walk the way of the cross?

The tragic and recent death of Princess Diana has had quite an incredible impact around the world. One of the interesting issues that arose was when they began to compare her to Mother Theresa. I was somewhat perplexed by the comparison. Princess Diana certainly did do some very positive things in her relatively short life but to compare her to Mother Theresa I felt was going a bit too far. Then a TV commentator summed it up for me when he said,

> 'The difference between the two is that Princess Diana was a princess who lived in a palace which she occasionally left to visit the poor and marginalised, whereas Mother Theresa was a nun who lived with the poor and marginalised and occasionally left that to visit princesses in palaces. There is a fundamental difference between the two.'

As I have reflected on this I have been challenged by the reality of this stark contrast. In truth, many of us desire to be like Princess Diana. We spend most of our Christian lives in comfort and occasionally leave it to do 'good' things that may even cost us something. Yet none of us could ever be a Princess Diana for we were not born into her lineage and position. Yet all of us could be a Mother Theresa who just obeyed her Lord and Master and chose to walk the way of the cross.

Jesus was fair and very clear; he calls us to lay down our lives. Self-preservation is one of the strongest instincts known to mankind, yet when applied to discipleship it can be a barrier to us giving ourselves to the war. Yet in war the cost must be counted, the decision must be made, our cross must be carried.

Fanatics for the Truth

One of the most vociferous and respected critics of William Booth was T.H. Huxley. He accused Booth of encouraging 'unchastened religious fanaticism.' He feared the impact of the Army's aggressive mission upon the 'intellect of the Nation' from Booth's 'organised fanaticism.' This slant, in truth, would probably have been seen by early Salvationists as a compliment if the true dictionary definition were used. The Collins Concise Dictionary describes this condition of the will as:

> 'Surpassing what is normal or accepted in enthusiasm for or belief in something.'

It goes on to describe a fanatic as:

> 'A person whose enthusiasm or zeal for something is extreme or beyond normal limits.'

Exactly. Now that is what I call a concise definition and precisely what it will take if we are to see this world transformed. Wars are won by people with a no-retreat, no-surrender mentality, no matter what the odds. Fanaticism is a condition of the will that engenders the kind of commitment needed to meet the challenges of bringing the gospel of Jesus to a world in such a mess.

A common objection to such thinking is that fanaticism is dangerous and needs to be avoided at all costs, yet I fear we miss the reality of the situation. Firstly, those conservative souls who would draw back at this would be those same people who are 'fanatical' about their sport, clothes, career and religious traditions. I have met those who would berate this perspective when preached and on the same day call for their corps officer or minister to be hung drawn and quartered for daring to change the order of service. I believe there is a fundamental difference between fanatical commitments to the 'forms' of a movement and the heart and vision of it. The former is often dangerous, lacking the authority of a biblical mandate, the latter essential for getting the job done.

Also those who would step back from such extreme perspectives, fail to appreciate history for it is only fanatical commitment that brought to birth so much of what we have inherited. It was the fanaticism of the martyred apostles that provided the soil of spiritual revolution that was to shape the future of the entire world. It was the fanaticism of Martin Luther as he stood before the assembled power of the Church, refusing to recant his beliefs knowing his life was at risk, that enabled him to recite the immortal words 'Here I stand. I can do no other, so help me God,' thereby beginning the Reformation. It was the fanaticism of the Wesley brothers that refused to bow before the pressure of the established church in seeking to reach the masses that brought Methodism to life. It was the fanaticism of the Booths that called for men and women who would be willing to 'die at their posts' that catapulted the Army onto the world scene, and I believe it is only that kind of fanatical commitment that will ensure our continued effectiveness in the world. To deny fanaticism is to deny our roots. To reject its heart, I believe, is to seal the doom of any movement like The Salvation Army, and indeed any Christian group wishing to make an impact on the world.

Balance

Many call for 'balance' at this stage. Balance is a correctional move in the context of uncontrolled anarchy. That is not our context as for most of us 'conservatism' is the order of the day. Balance in that context is merely a recipe for the continuance of the comfortable status quo and eventual rigor mortis of institutional death. As George Verwer, founder of Operation Mobilisation says:

> 'It is easier to calm down a fanatic than it is to raise the dead.'

Balance and 'being sound' have become labels of identity that some of us wear. They have taken on almost canonical authority and become the benchmarks for much of the Church to measure the acceptability of people and projects. This position must be questioned and exposed for the compromised sham it is. God the Father, sending his 'only begotten Son' to be brutalised, to have half his back shredded off, to have stakes driven into his wrists and feet, and a spear driven into his side can hardly be described as balanced. **The mentality of a man who willingly embraced such abuse and then said, *'As the Father has sent me, I am sending you'* (John 20:21) can hardly be described as sound.**

Conservatism never changed anything, least of all a world in the desperate situation that we find it in today. No, only a return to our fanatical roots will get the job done in the same way it gave birth to the movement. Early Salvationists did not 'belong' to the Army but were 'possessed' by its spirit and passion.

Here is just a taste of their heart:

> 'My heart is cheered. We are making the devil mad. Victory will come! Look out for some martyrdom here in the near future – it is to come, sure. Well, we are saved to die and don't care much where our bones are buried.'[54]

> 'Here is a war in which you will win celestial honours, honours that will last for ever. Will you enlist? We take all recruits in this Army. If you have a **heart to love**, come along. We want men and women indifferent to

all other aims and ends but the extension of the Kingdom of Jesus.'[55]

'Owing to our adherence to this rigid military system, we are losing almost every year officers, as well as people, who, having lost their first love, begin to hanker after the "rights," "privileges," "comforts," "teaching" or "respectability of the churches." No one remains with us, or is likely to remain, whose sole object in life is not the attainment of the one purpose ever kept before the Army: the rescue from sin and Hell of those who are farthest from God...'[56]

'We want the burning love to dying men which feels with a terrible pang every sinner's misery, and forgets danger and difficulty and discouragement in the deathless agony to pluck brands from the burning. We want to be bigger, grander, holier, more God-like men and women, and we must be if we are to do what God expects of us.'[57]

One of the most frustrating and draining aspects of leadership at any level is when good people leave your organisation. One of the greatest tragedies of contemporary Salvation Army history is when quality, committed and fanatical people leave this Movement not because we are too extreme and ask too much. No, it is often because they are strangled by a conservatism more committed to protecting outdated religious systems than to reaching lost people. Can there be a more destructive barrier to re-discovering our founding dream? Tony Campolo often speaks of the perspective consistently propagated by conservative religious institutions:

'We are in danger of losing the young not because we ask too much of them, but because we ask too little.'

It is true that within Salvation Army circles a great deal of time is required of the young who get wrapped up in our existing programmes, but often they fulfil these expectations on auto pilot; it draws little from them. We need challenges that cause people to dig to the very depths of who they are, stepping out, risking like never before. That is an organisation worth belonging to.

Definition of Terms

What I am not calling for is a blind, unthinking fanaticism that refuses to be sensitive to people or situations, nor a religious bigotry that rejects people as well as their beliefs. What I am holding up is a kind of 'thinking' fanaticism. This is a thought-through decision of the will. It recognises the heinous reality of the situation in which we find ourselves and commits to uncompromising dedication to do anything to see things change. Nothing short of this kind of devotion and lived-out commitment will push forward our Kingdom agenda in the way that is required.

From those who would question the use of such terms as unthinking I would question their own analysis. To think that anything other than this kind of response is adequate to meet the challenge of our day, is to avoid completely the reality of our world. It is they who I would suggest are unthinking.

I was challenged recently reading Jim Wallis's book, *Soul of Politics* whereby he reflects on the verse *'blessed are the peace makers.'* It was not those that just prayed for peace nor held it up as a conceptual idea but rather those who lived out lives of 'peacemakers.' He saw that he needed to be as sacrificially committed to the making of peace, as were those committed to violence and injustice.

Fanatical warriors are those who are even more intensely committed to bringing about the peace than those committed to waging war against this world. In the film *First Knight*, one of the best lines defining our warfare role comes to the fore when King Arthur states:

'There is a peace that is only found on the other side of war.'

It is those who within their will are committed to waging a war of love with a fanatical intensity that will be the heroes of our world. It has always been that way. Not all the high-profile types, but rather the majority of unsung heroes of Christendom who have faithfully and fanatically served and sacrificed.

Theology of Fanaticism

A key aspect of this battle of the will is the theological mindset with which we approach the challenges before us. To sustain a fanatical commitment we will require that victorious perspective of what I call 'So what?' theology. The kind of theology that no matter the odds or opposition has such a confidence in the adequacy of God that you keep pushing for victory.

It's that David versus Goliath thinking that hears 'He's so big' yet replies **'So what?'** 'It's never been done before.' 'So what?' 'There are too many of them.' 'So what?' 'We don't have the money.' 'So what?' 'The odds are just stacked against us, everyone has always failed before, the challenge is just so great.' 'So what, so what, so what?' If God is for us it doesn't matter who is against us (Romans 8:31). With Christ I can do all things (Philippians 4:13). I am capable of more than I can imagine or even dream of because of his power that is that is at work within me (Ephesians 3:20), for I am filled with the same Spirit that raised Jesus from the dead (Romans 8:11), so I can be bold, strong and courageous, for I know that the Lord, my God will be with me wherever I go (Joshua 1:9). That is the theology of 'So what?' An essential for fanatical warriors.

Surely, the sceptics say, this is just closing our eyes to the real situation, blind faith exposed as a sham in the face of reality. Tell that to the disciples on resurrection morning. No matter what the 'real situation' there is always a greater reality that transcends all others, the reality of a sovereign, all-powerful God. As Billy Graham said when asked about miracles in the Bible:

> 'Because the Bible begins *"In the beginning God created..."* I would have believed it if it had said that Jonah had swallowed the whale!'

The tragedy of liberal thinking and theology that has stripped the Bible of so much of its power in people's minds, is that it bases its thinking on the crumbling edifice of rationalism. A no-hope leap into the philosophical dark with nothing to say to a desperate world living with the consequences of reality.

The fanaticism of the Early Church, early Army and contemporary explosive Pentecostal growth in Asia, Africa and Latin America, was and is carried forward on a tidal wave of confidence in the power of God to answer the call and need of the day.

Conclusion

As I have read through this script a particular thought has continually filtered through my mind – 'You're crazy.' This is too extreme, too intense, totally over the top and immensely unbalanced. This may be no surprise to those of you who know me but I have personally found it very challenging for a number of reasons. Firstly, I don't live it. These are the ideals I want to live for, the dreams I wish to dream and the lifestyle I wish to model, yet too often I fall short. I, like all of you, echo the words of the apostle Paul who did the things he didn't want to do and didn't do the things he wanted to do. He, like me and you, came to the call of discipleship in weakness, yet that does nothing to lessen the call to absolute obedience and surrender to which God calls us.

Secondly, we are all on journeys, all at different stages, all having come from different places. Again, when feeling inadequate, we should take comfort from the same thing that brought comfort to Paul:

> *'My grace is sufficient for you, for my power is made perfect in weakness.'*   (2 Corinthians 12:9)

But again the feeling of inadequacy must not paralyse us into inactivity or defeatism; there is a war on. Our response could be like that of David when facing Goliath. As a good friend of mine says, David could have thought, 'Oh Lord he's so big, I'm going to die!' or he could have thought, 'Oh Lord he's so big, how can I miss!' Whichever he thought, he like us, had a decision to make.

This decision, I think, is at the heart of the whole issue discussed in this book. The primary issue is to ask, 'Who am I?' or more accurately, 'Who will I be?' The Salvation Army of which I am a part is merely a metaphor. It has no value in itself, no special place in the heart of God. I personally find it quite offensive when I hear of people talking about the 'good old Army' in slushy sentimental terms, then deny its passion by their compromise and shallow religiosity. To do so misses its heart, betrays its Founders, and prostitutes its true purpose for self-centred agendas. It is just a metaphor that finds its definition in people and the lives they live individually and corporately. It is these lives, these living testimonies that give it its definition and that hold before us an awesome responsibility.

Graham Kendrick, the song writer, lifts up the image of all of the unanswered prayers of William and Catherine Booth and all the unfulfilled promises God made to them that would be the rightful inheritance of their children. Not those necessarily of bloodline nor organisational line but their 'passion children.' These are those who rightfully claim their birthright by the vision they share and the surrendered lives they live. The issue of identity that will be established in a celestial court is a simple one. Will we pay the price of what it will mean to be a rightful heir, a passion child of this metaphorical dream?

Many of us who would aspire to claim such an inheritance, have never seen the metaphor truly lived, it has merely been recited in the stories told and proclaimed in the preachers rhetoric, and recorded in the historian's pages. Yet when we have heard, listened and read, we have caught a taste. By the wind of the Spirit we have been captured by its passion and infected by its still yet unfulfilled dreams. It is to these that we must give ourselves as the outworking of our obedience to Christ, claiming that as yet unseen, being drawn by its magnetism and power.

I watched in disbelief the news programme, profiling the horror of the Lebanese suicide bombers. Each of them barely in their teens, each carrying their Kalashnikov rifle, their chests covered with the would-be medals of heroism in the form of plastic explosive. They were paraded up and down by a bearded 'sergeant major', himself holding his rifle high and filling their minds with cries of patriotism and revolution. The correspondent, now talking to this leader of the would-be assassins who was identified as the refugee leader of this disenfranchised people driven from their homes many years before, struggled to hide her disbelief. She questioned him, asking why these children would give their lives for a land they had never visited or even seen, a place they would probably never go to. The leader replied through the translator with words I will never forget:

> 'Lady, none of us have ever been to Palestine, but when the west wind blows we smell it in the air, and for that we will live and die!'

There is a war on. It needs to be fought by men and women who will strive to win the battles for their hearts, minds and wills. Our peace will only be found on the other side of this war. Its battlefield includes every corner of the earth. The stakes are eternally high. There is a dream for a victory already won but not yet fully claimed. Will we fight, will we claim our birthright, will we answer the need of our day, will we give ourselves for the sake of the faceless yet priceless millions of our world?

> While thousands starve, will we fight?
> While our planet dies, will I fight?
> While children are abused and butchered, will you
>   fight?
> While millions are lost in darkness will you fight?
> While the battle rages on will you fight, will you fight
>   and fight to the very end?

Post Script

> Are you tired, brace yourself
> Have you wearied, strengthen yourself
> Have you forgotten, remember
> The revolution is not yet over.
>   (Bolshevik Revolutionary Poem)

Bibliography

1. Bramwell Booth, Autograph of 'Every land is my Fatherland', *The Officers' Review*, 1941, p. 255

2. Major John Rhemick, *A New People of God*, The Salvation Army, 10 W. Algonquin Road, Des Plaines, Illinois 60016, p. 51

3. Major John Rhemick, *A New People of God*, The Salvation Army, 10 W. Algonquin Road, Des Plaines, Illinois 60016, p. 80

4. Colonel Phil Needham, *Community in Mission*, The Salvation Army, p. 72

5. A selection of the writings of William Booth arranged by Cyril J. Barnes, *The Founder Speaks Again*, Salvationist Publishing and Supplies Ltd, London, p. 100

6. A selection of the writings of William Booth arranged by Cyril J. Barnes, *The Founder Speaks Again*, Salvationist Publishing and Supplies Ltd, London, p. 39

7. Catherine Booth, *Agressive Christianity*, The Salvation Army, p. 9

8. William Booth, *The Founder's Messages to Soldiers*, The Salvation Army, p. 126

9. Bramwell Booth, *Echoes and Memories*, Hodder & Stoughton, pp. 67–8

10. Major John Rhemick, *A New People of God*, The Salvation Army, 10 W. Algonquin Road, Des Plaines, Illinois 60016, p. 69

11. Charles Dickens, *Bleak House*, Oxford University Press, p. 647

12. Catherine Booth, *Godliness*, The Salvation Army, p. 148. Re-printed Salvation Army Supplies, 1424 Northeast Expressway, Atlanta, Georgia, 30329

13. Major John Rhemick, *A New People of God*, The Salvation Army, 10 W. Algonquin Road, Des Plaines, Illinois 60016, p. 176

14. Roger Green, *War on Two Fronts*, Salvation Army Publishing & Supplies Ltd, 1989, p. 82

15. William Booth, *In Darkest England and the Way Out*, Salvation Army Publishing & Supplies Ltd, 1890, p. 16

16. William Booth, *Salvation for Both Worlds*, Salvationist Publishing & Supplies Ltd, 1890, pp. 2–3

17. William Booth, *The Founder's Messages to Soldiers*, The Salvation Army, p. 177

18. Major John Rhemick, *A New People of God*, The Salvation Army, 10 W. Algonquin Road, Des Plaines, Illinois 60016, p. 78

19. Major John Rhemick, *A New People of God*, The Salvation Army, 10 W. Algonquin Road, Des Plaines, Illinois 60016, p. 122

20. Major John Rhemick, *A New People of God*, The Salvation Army, 10 W. Algonquin Road, Des Plaines, Illinois 60016, p. 68

21. A selection of the writings of William Booth arranged by Cyril J. Barnes, *The Founder Speaks Again*, Salvationist Publishing and Supplies Ltd, London, p. 49

22. Major John Rhemick, *A New People of God*, The Salvation Army, 10 W. Algonquin Road, Des Plaines, Illinois 60016, p. 158

23. Evangeline Booth, *The Song Book of The Salvation Army*, The Salvation Army, p. 665

24. John Newton, *The Song Book of The Salvation Army*, Salvationist Publishing and Supplies Ltd, p. 247

25. Donald B. Kraybill, *The Upside Down Kingdom*, Herald Press, p. 19

26. Tom Sine, *Taking Discipleship Seriously*, Triangle Books, p. 40

27. Tom Sine, *Taking Discipleship Seriously*, Triangle Books, p. 23

28. Jim Wallis, *The Call to Conversion*, Triangle Books, p. 40

29. *The Salvation Army Handbook of Doctrine*, Salvationist Publishing and Supplies Ltd, p. 9

30. Os Guinness, *Fit Bodies Fat Minds*, Hodder & Stoughton, p. 9

31. Os Guinness, *Fit Bodies Fat Minds*, Hodder & Stoughton, p. 10

32. Os Guinness, *Fit Bodies Fat Minds*, Hodder & Stoughton, p. 134

33. Os Guinness, *Fit Bodies Fat Minds*, Hodder & Stoughton, p. 136

34. Os Guinness, *Fit Bodies Fat Minds*, Hodder & Stoughton, p. 141

35. Os Guinness, *Fit Bodies Fat Minds*, Hodder & Stoughton, p. 141

36. Os Guinness, *Fit Bodies Fat Minds*, Hodder & Stoughton, p. 151

37. Richard Collier, *The General Next to God*, Collins, pp. 175–6

38. Tom Sine, *Wild Hope*, Monarch Publications Ltd, p. 84

39. Dietrich Bonhoeffer, *The Cost of Discipleship*, SCM Press Ltd, p. 155

40. Richard Foster, *Freedom of Simplicity*, Triangle/SPCK, Holy Trinity Church, London, p. 4

41. The Salvation Army Mission Team, *Mission Quarterly (MQ)*, issue 5, p. 10

42. Richard Foster, *Freedom of Simplicity*, Triangle/SPCK, Holy Trinity Church, London, p. 10

43. Richard Foster, *Freedom of Simplicity*, Triangle/SPCK, Holy Trinity Church, London, p. 20

44. Richard Foster, *Freedom of Simplicity*, Triangle/SPCK, Holy Trinity Church, London, p. 110

45. *The Works of John Milton*, The Wordsworth Poetry Library, published 1994

46. Melody Green and David Hazarel, *No Compromise – The Life Story of Keith Green*, 1989, Word

47. David Watson, *Discipleship*, Hodder & Stoughton, p. 19

48. *The Song Book of The Salvation Army*, International Headquarters, p. 380

49. Major John Rhemick, *A New People of God*, The Salvation Army, 10 W. Algonquin Road, Des Plaines, Illinois 60016, p. 71

50. *The Independent*, 20.05.96

51. Rob Frost, *Which Way for the Church?*, Kingsway Publications Ltd, p. 98

52. Colonel Phil Needham, *Community in Mission*, The Salvation Army, pp. 41–2

53. Corretta Scott King, *The Words of Martin Luther King*, Collins Fount Paperbacks, p. 23

54. Major John Rhemick, *A New People of God*, The Salvation Army, 10 W. Algonquin Road, Des Plaines, Illinois 60016, p. 79

55. Major John Rhemick, *A New People of God*, The Salvation Army, 10 W. Algonquin Road, Des Plaines, Illinois 60016, p. 68

56. Major John Rhemick, *A New People of God*, The Salvation Army, 10 W. Algonquin Road, Des Plaines, Illinois 60016, p. 79

57. Major John Rhemick, *A New People of God*, The Salvation Army, 10 W. Algonquin Road, Des Plaines, Illinois 60016, p. 65

Appendix I

Other Resources

Care for the Family, *Make Love Last*,
published by Make Love Last, sponsored by Care Trust

Steve Chalke, *Lessons in Love Video Package*,
published by Care for the Family

Chick Yuill, *And God Created Sex*, published by Monarch

John White, *Eros Defiled*, published by IVP

Appendix II

Officership

It would be inappropriate not to mention this specific area of vocation in a book so focused on the mission and ministry of The Salvation Army. Full-time officership was Booth's pragmatic response to his need for missioners who could travel around the country opening up new centres of outreach and resourcing existing ones. I am sure the current-day scenario of long-term pastors, specialist social care ministry and numerous administrative roles was far from his mind.

For many of my officer, friends and family much more thinking is needed in terms of a theology of officership and the philosophy of ministry, for them to come to terms with the new context. Space does not allow for such a debate within this book and also I would not be qualified to write it. What I do want to do in what follows is to address some of the challenges facing this form of vocation, affirm its unique and essential role within The Salvation Army and challenge all those reading this book to consider this for themselves.

Changing World

The world has changed dramatically since the phenomena of officership began. For many underclass people it provided the only career they would have had. For most, if not all, women this was certainly so; very few wives would have had any expectation of a career. It emerged in a world that expected people to give their lives to one profession for the whole of their working life. Thus it made sense to ask for a lifetime commitment to the specific role of officership. Officers became the ubiquitous generalists who fulfilled every role which went well beyond the original missioner expectation.

Things have changed dramatically since then. Many of those coming in are highly skilled, qualified people who have already fulfilled a significant role in a particular field. This includes many women who have led their own career distinct from their husband's role. The nature of employment has changed dramatically whereby young people expect to have two or three career moves during their lifetime, very few sticking with one sphere of work. This is not so much caused by lack of commitment of those involved but it has just become the expected norm. Increasing numbers of young people who are deeply committed to The Salvation Army, are seeking out opportunities as full-time employees within specialist niche roles, as opposed to generalist ministry.

These are just some of the challenges officership faces, predominantly within the Western world. The extent to which officership is able to respond creatively to these will, I feel, largely determine its future.

The Role

My own view, whilst accepting its limited value, is the recognition of officership once again as a specialist role. Firstly, in the arena of leadership.

Ephesians chapter four lays out very clearly the role of people gifted in a particular way; some to be apostles, some to be prophets, some to be evangelists, and some to be pastors and teachers, to prepare God's people for works of service, so that the body of Christ may be built up

(Ephesians 4:11–12). The meaning seems very clear that those with the gifts mentioned are primarily responsible not for 'doing the work' but for equipping the saints for doing just that. This is quite difficult for an evangelist and activist (and some would say hyperactive evangelist) like myself who loves to be involved in the 'hands on' stuff. Yet Scripture seems quite clear that leaders gifted in the ways described have a primary function to equip others to do the work. The calling of officership, if seen as aligned to this leadership role, must be this essential equipping of the saints.

Many of my officer friends see this as their primary role to lead, envision and equip their people for the work of ministry. This role needs to be affirmed and its value as a specialist role esteemed in the appropriate way. This must also include leadership at a divisional and territorial level that fulfils more of an apostolic, overseeing function supporting the front-line grass-roots ministry.

The other essential role is obviously that of specialist social carers. For those gifted in terms of their compassion, empathy and service to care for those with specific needs, officership is an essential role. With the statutory social services downsizing throughout the Western world, and with much more responsibility being passed on to the voluntary sector, this is a role that will increase in need and significance.

The financial implications of full-time local corps leadership is significant with 70% of corps in the UK and over 90% of corps in the USA in receipt of centralised grant funding. Morally this position is not tenable. The public give us money to care for the needy, not to keep our heating and lighting on during winter. Living in a world where the needs are increasing rapidly, and a Church where the giving is static or shrinking, full-time leadership may become a thing of the past for most of our small to medium corps. A form of part-time/job share officership may be the shape of things to come.

The Challenge

Whatever the future of officership in a changing world there are some realities that need to be faced. Firstly, officership needs to be brought into the market place of vocational choices rather than being perceived as some special elitist calling. From my experience of working with young people, an oft-times one-track vocational theology that is neither biblical or true Salvation Army has closed their minds to the possibility of a fulfilling ministry as a Salvation Army officer. It needs to be affirmed as the role it is, for those gifted in the appropriate ways. Whilst it remains on the fringes, accessible only to those with a powerful 'call', it will remain inaccessible for the consideration of most. By giving officership a kudos above and beyond other calls we inhibit rather than enhance its development and growth.

Secondly, the nature of leadership is changing dramatically in the Western world. To say that top-down hierarchical leadership is dead is an understatement. Current specialists in leadership such as Charles Handy and Professor John Hunt of the London Business School, suggest that linear and relational leadership will shape future organisations, and emerging generations will have little attraction to heavily authoritarian institutions.

Thirdly, we obviously need more candidates entering the training college than are at present doing so. With The Salvation Army strategically placed in many nations around the world to be the most significant vehicle of hope and benevolence, this is an exciting time to take on the responsibility of leadership. Our increasingly secularised societies are turning their backs on institutional religion and are cynical about politicians and macro organisations. In this context those who will be looked to for a lead, are people with a robust and earthy spirituality and their sleeves rolled up to face the challenges of the world. The demographics of officership in many nations means that significant levels of responsibility will be held by those of younger generations. The opportunity to shape the future of this movement in terms of its leadership has possibly never been greater.

Fourthly, all of us within full-time Christian leadership must make sure we keep mission at the forefront of our thinking and lives. The challenge for people like myself and many of my officer-friends is to ensure that we are doing our all to inspire and equip people to wage this war and also to ensure that we ourselves are engaging with people who do not have living faith. Many ministers and officers I have met confessed to not even being on first name terms with their neighbours let alone being actively involved in reaching them. This snare of being consumed within the affairs of a Christian subculture must be avoided at all costs. There is a fundamental difference between striving to be professional in our Christian ministry which must be encouraged, and becoming a professional Christian who is paid to follow Jesus. This must be rejected for the sin that it is.

People employed by the Church are constantly in danger of settling into the comfort of the fold. I am constantly challenged by how little risk is involved in my current role. The extent to which I need to step out and trust God for provision seems to decrease annually. It is interesting to note that in China where the underground house churches run church-planting courses – which include a module of how to undergo interrogation and torture by the authorities without releasing information – they have people in their hundreds queuing to get on the course. Whereas in the West many Bible colleges and even our own training colleges, struggle to recruit people with all the 'benefits' held up in the publicity.

The debate about the theology of officership, the call and leadership, will continue well into the future. As already noted, more leaders are needed than are currently within our training colleges, so for this movement to fulfil its God-given potential, it needs leaders of quality to take responsibility to serve in this way.

What is apparent, is that for someone to become an officer when God's best for them is to stay in their working role, or vice versa, would be sin. Yet for me the issue is not so much the theology of officership but rather our theology of mission and where we perceive its focus to be. We must avoid at all costs the internal workings of our religious system to consume all of our best time, energy and resources. Our vocational appeals at youth councils must truly reflect our theology of the priesthood and maximise the opportunity to encourage, equip and inspire people to be their best for God wherever he has placed them. I believe the Great Commission forces us to consider afresh how we might better be reaching people in all spheres of society. Decisions of the will must be determined by individuals within communities deciding how best they can impact this world for God. Lift up vision and vocation and the Spirit will guide you to the specific sphere.

Glossary

Articles of War: A statement of belief and practice signed by those becoming 'soldiers' in The Salvation Army.

Candidate: Someone who has offered to become an officer in The Salvation Army, and who has been accepted by the Army for this role, but who has yet to go through the process of training for the ministry of officership.

Corps: A local Salvation Army church.

Council of War: A specially convened meeting of officers to discuss issues pertinent to the mission of The Salvation Army.

Envoy: Someone who fulfils a role similar to that of an Officer, but who has not been ordained and commissioned in the same way as an officer. An envoy will often be the leader of a local corps.

Officer: An ordained and commissioned minister who works full-time for The Salvation Army, either in charge of a corps, or in a leadership position at a local, regional, national or international level.

Salvationist: Someone who attends The Salvation Army.

Soldier: A member of The Salvation Army who has accepted the beliefs of the Army and who has signed the Articles of War. Soldiers may wear the uniform if they wish.

If you have enjoyed this book and would like to help us to send a copy of it and many other titles to needy pastors in the **Third World**, please write for further information or send your gift to:

Sovereign World Trust
PO Box 777, Tonbridge
Kent TN11 0ZS
United Kingdom

or to the **'Sovereign World'** distributor in your country.